✣

Seventeen Steps
to Heaven

Leo J. Trese

Seventeen Steps to Heaven

A Catholic Guide to Salvation

SOPHIA INSTITUTE PRESS®
Manchester, New Hampshire

Seventeen Steps to Heaven: A Catholic Guide to Salvation is a new edition of *Everyman's Road to Heaven* (Notre Dame, Indiana: Fides Publishers, 1961). Chapter 11 has been abridged, and minor editorial revisions have been made throughout.

Sophia Institute Press®
Box 5284, Manchester, NH 03108
1-800-888-9344
www.sophiainstitute.com

Nihil obstat: Louis J. Putz, C.S.C.
University of Notre Dame
Imprimatur: Leo A. Pursley, D.D.
Bishop of Fort Wayne-South Bend, Indiana

Library of Congress Cataloging-in-Publication Data

Trese, Leo J. (Leo John), 1902-
    Seventeen steps to heaven : a Catholic guide to salvation / Leo J. Trese.
        p.   cm.
    Rev. ed. of: Everyman's road to heaven. 1961.
    ISBN 1-928832-26-1 (pbk. : alk. paper)
    1. Spiritual life — Catholic Church. 2. Catholic Church — Doctrines. 3. Salvation. I. Trese, Leo J. (Leo John), 1902- Everyman's road to heaven. II. Title.

BX2350.2.T718 2001
248.4'82 — dc21   2001020806

01 02 03 04 05 10 9 8 7 6 5 4 3 2

Contents

❧

Biographical Note

Seventeen Steps
to Heaven

Editor's note: The biblical quotations in the following pages are taken from the Confraternity Version of the Old and New Testaments. Where applicable, biblical quotations have been cross-referenced with the differing names and enumeration in the Revised Standard Version, using the following symbol: (RSV =).

Chapter One

❧

Deepen your understanding of the Faith

＄

How many times have you thought of God today? At least once, it is to be hoped, as you said your morning prayers. If you live within hearing distance of an *Angelus* bell[1] or passed a church, perhaps your thoughts turned to God once or twice more. But is that often enough?

Those whom we love are never far beneath the surface of our thoughts. Their images keep constantly breaking through to the surface. If you are married, for example, how often have you thought of your husband or wife today? If you are a parent, how often have you thought of your children? The chances are that you cannot even count the number of times. If you are a young man or woman in love, the thought of your beloved is probably so dominant as to interfere at times with the ordinary business of living.

It seems strange, then, that God does not come in for a greater share of our thoughts. He is infinitely lovable, the only Being who can completely exhaust the human heart's capacity

[1] A bell rung three times a day to call the faithful to pray the *Angelus*, a prayer that recalls the Incarnation.

for love. We accept this truth with our minds. We accept also the fact that we ought to love God with our whole mind, heart, soul, and strength, above all other beings. Time and again we tell God that we do so love Him. Yet hours can pass, a whole day can pass, without our mind once turning to God. There is a wide gap here between theory and practice.

This divergence between theory and practice becomes even more puzzling when we consider that loving God is the most important business of our lives. God is the whole reason for my existence. He created me because He wants to have me with Him for all eternity, in a union with Him that will spell an utter ecstasy of happiness for me. A few years of so-called life flash by in this world, then I begin my real life with God — provided that I have prepared myself for it. And the only preparation required of me is that, here and now, I begin and grow in love for God. This is the real business, the sole business of human existence. Yet if a merchant gave as little thought to his business as most of us give to loving God, he soon would be bankrupt.

However, we must not exaggerate this point. We know that our love for God is measured by how hard we try to keep His commandments and do His will, not merely by how often we think of Him. We also know that our love for God differs from love for humans, in that love for God does not, usually, affect our emotions the way human love does. It is probably to be expected that an emotional love will push itself into consciousness more often than a love, however strong, that is seated in the mind and will alone. Yet, conceding all this, it does seem that God gets a rather meager share of our attention.

Deepen your understanding of the Faith

❧

Daily pressures can distract you from God

One reason for this is that God tends to get crowded out of our minds by the thousand and one distractions of everyday living. There are so many things we have to do and so many things we want to do. There are so many plans to be made, so many details to be attended to. We get up in the morning, and, even as we say our morning prayers, half of our mind is on something else. "I must remember to have the washer fixed." "I must get the oil changed in the car today." "I wonder whether the boss will still be sore at me this morning." God gets His short and divided minute, then we rush through our day with no further thought for Him until, with a series of yawns, we give Him another divided minute at our bedside that night. It isn't always this way, of course, and it isn't this way with everybody. But it is this way too often with too many of us.

Fortunately, God is patient. If He sees us making a reasonable effort to live our lives in union with Him, He is willing to wait for eternity to get — as He then will — our full attention. Still, we dare not presume upon God's patience. There is always the grave danger that inattention to God may lead to forgetfulness of His rights. There is danger that the world may engulf us so completely that God will become unimportant and His will irrelevant to our conduct. There is danger, in other words, that what began as inadvertence to God may end in disobedience to God — may end in sin.

Even if our laxity does not reach the unhappy climax of sin, there still is the tragedy of wasted hours and days that have not been lived for God. Our lives should be lived on a supernatural level. This means that, in addition to being in the state of grace, we have the habitual intention (frequently renewed) of performing all our actions for God and in accordance with His will. If our life has this supernatural orientation, everything we do — whether it is changing the diaper on the baby or changing the tire on the car — has value in God's eyes and gains merit for us in Heaven. Lived in union with God, our whole life becomes a continual prayer. The demands of duty may keep God from our conscious mind a great part of the time, but He remains the focus of all our activity. Every thought, word, and action has been predirected to Him.

To one who loves God, there is a sadness in the sight of so many people — good people, too — who habitually live their lives on a purely natural level. These are people who seem to have a natural sense of decency and rightness. They have an inborn kindness and spirit of helpfulness. They are truthful, honest in their business dealings, and faithful to their family duties. Yet there is no thought of God in what they do. They live uprightly because this is the only kind of life that gives them satisfaction. If you asked them the reason for their virtue, they might answer, "I owe it to myself to be a decent, law-abiding person."

There is real tragedy here, in these lives that remain unmotivated by love for God, in this natural virtue that gains no merit in Heaven. It is tragedy triply compounded if we, who know better, waste our days and dissipate our spiritual wealth through thoughtlessness toward God. Yet, if we do nothing to resist the pressure, the demands of our innumerable daily duties *can* make us forget God.

In addition to such pressures, we have to contend also with the downhill drag of our fallen human nature. Original Sin has made the practice of virtue an arduous task. In human affairs, it is an exceptional person who can stay at an exacting job for a long time without gradually slowing up, taking it a little easier. In spiritual matters, this inclination to slow up is even more universal. Who of us has not had the experience of making bold and noble resolutions to conquer this fault or practice this virtue, only to find, at the end of a month or a year, that he is right back where he started from? After several such failures we may be tempted to discouragement and to give up the struggle entirely. Yet that, we know, is not the answer.

Renew your understanding
and practice of the Faith

What is the answer? We might glibly say that the answer lies in making better use of prayer and the sacraments in order to acquire greater spiritual strength. The defect of this answer is that it does not go deep enough. A better use of prayer and the sacraments may be the very point on which we have often resolved and poorly persevered. Prayer and the sacraments surely are an answer, but we must look for "an answer behind the answer."

To make better use of prayer and the sacraments and thus to experience healthy spiritual growth, we need to understand and to appreciate these means of grace. This understanding and appreciation needs continual renewal. Just as a neglected table becomes filmed over with dust from we-know-not-where, so also does our sense of the supernatural become gradually obscured and dulled. Periodically we must revive our understanding of the nature and the effects of prayer and the sacraments — the wonder of them and the tremendous power of them.

Still another need we have: a need for a renewal of our motivation, a recharging of our spiritual batteries. The force within us that impels us to choose good over evil, the better over the merely good, God over self, needs refreshing. For this we must return to a consideration of those basic truths of religion which provide the motive power for all spiritual progress. The purpose of life, the irresistible attraction of Heaven, the malice of sin, the repulsive horror of Hell, the inescapable fact of death and our awful responsibility as we face God in judgment — these are the basic truths. They are the truths that urge us onward and counteract our human tendency to "take it easy." Unfortunately, they are truths whose full significance, once known, we too easily forget — in fact, almost willingly forget. Yet we dare not let ourselves forget them. Our eternity hangs upon their freshness in our minds and hearts.

These, then, are our twin needs: to renew our appreciation of things spiritual and to re-present to ourselves the foundation truths of all spirituality. To satisfy these needs is the purpose of retreats and parish missions. To minister to these needs is the aim of every priest who preaches. Yet it is seldom more than once a year that we can make a retreat or mission. The Sunday sermon comes to us weekly, but the limitation of time allows it a very narrow scope.

Deepen your understanding of the Faith

This is why the truly practical Catholic, the Catholic who takes seriously his vocation to love God, will try to make spiritual reading a regular part of his weekly, if not daily, program. The purpose of such reading is to gain inspiration rather than instruction. For most of us, it is not so much a case of increasing our knowledge as it is of going back to what we already know. The shelves of our Catholic bookstores and libraries are loaded with books that can give new meaning and direction to our lives.

With the faith and goodwill we bring to such reading, God's grace inevitably will be at work. In the recollection or discovery of old truths we shall find the springboard to a freshened and intensified love for God. And love Him we must, or we perish.

Chapter Two

Strive to do God's will in all things

§

The director of a proposed "supercolossal" movie was engaged in the task of choosing an actress for the leading part in the picture. He sat at his desk with dozens of photographs spread out before him that had been supplied by various theatrical agents who were seeking the part for a client. Eventually the director put his finger on one photograph and said to his secretary, "There is exactly the type I want. Phone the woman, and get her in here."

It is quite a jump from Hollywood to Heaven, from a movie director to God. Yet we have here an example, however inadequate, of the reason for your existence. Back in the limitless reaches of eternity (speaking in human terms), God made His plans for the universe and did the casting for all the parts that must be filled, down to the end of time. In His divine mind He looked over the pictures of all the souls, limitless in number, whom He could create. When he came to the image of you, He stopped and said, "This is a person who moves me to love. This is a person I want with me through all eternity. This is the person, too, whom I need for a special part in my plan. This is a soul I shall create."

It is only in human imagery, always inadequate, that we are able to talk about God and His actions. However, allowing for the inadequacies of our expression, this is a description of what really did happen. God made you because you evoked His love more than a billion other possible souls whose images were in His divine mind. And even though there were other souls He might have loved equally well, there was a part in His plan, a job that needed doing, that no one else could fulfill quite as well as you. So God made *you*, rather than one of the other billion "possibles."

⁂

Live always to fulfill God's plan for you

This conviction as to the purposefulness of our lives is what we call the Christian sense of vocation. It is the awareness that we are called to fill a special spot in this world and to be a unique object of God's love, both here and hereafter. It is the vivid, day-to-day realization that we matter to God; that we are not just one of several billion souls tossed off by God in an absent-minded moment of creativity; that we have an individual importance to God and that God has a personal, intense, almost anxious interest in us.

Our Christian vocation imposes on us the obligation to justify God's love for us, God's hopes for us. We do so when we try, day by day, to do God's will to the best of our ability. This means that we make God's will our compass, the norm and the guide of our lives. In all our decisions and in all our choices, "what God would want me to do," must take precedence over "what I would like to do."

Strive to do God's will in all things

This does not mean necessarily that God's will and mine will always be in conflict. Quite frequently, God gets us to do His will precisely by making it attractive to us; by letting us think that the course of action He wants is one that we have gladly chosen for ourselves. But conflicts there will be, and, anytime God's will lies in a different direction, we must be ready to surrender our own preferences instantly. This is the one infallible proof of our love for God; this is what justifies His love for us.

This unswerving attachment to God's will also is what justifies God's choice of us for His work. We rarely know what the particular job is for which God has chosen us — a job that no one else could do quite as well as we. It may be a certain person whom God can reach with His grace only through us. It may be some chain of events that only we can initiate or some evil that only we can avert.

In most instances, we shall not know, until eternity, what particular task it was for which we — and we alone — were best fitted. This is another and urgent reason why we must strive, day after day, to do God's will in little things as well as in big things. We do not know which of our actions will be our exclusive and essential contribution to God's plan, or which of our words will be the fateful words upon which God is depending.

We know only that we must face each day and each moment as though *this* were the day and *this* the moment. Otherwise we run the risk of failing God in the one thing that so greatly determined His choice of us; and in failing God, we shall fail ourselves.

❈

Find your personal worth in your
special calling from God

Our Christian vocation carries responsibility, but it has its compensations, too. One such compensation is the wholesome feeling of personal worth that should be mine. If I am important to God, I am indeed an important person. Other people may not rate me very highly. My talents may be quite limited, and to those who know me, I may be just an average sort of person. My job may be a relatively humble one, and I may be tempted to feel inferior as I see others around me making their mark in the world. Then I remember that money, position, and popularity — all the yardsticks by which the world measures success — are to God nothing more than a child's playthings. Eventually they must be cast aside and left behind.

In the meantime, if I am in a state of grace and am following God's will as my road map through life, then every least action of mine has an everlasting value. However lowly the world may esteem me, every breath I draw is precious to God. Speaking again in human terms, God made me because He needs me. There is something that has to be done that only I can do. What greater personal worth could there be than to be needed by God? It matters little that I do not know the nature of my essential role in God's plan. It is enough to know that I am as valuable to God as the most distinguished person the world has ever acclaimed.

This sense of personal worth is not pride. It is not even vanity. Pride consists in declaring my independence of God, as though I alone were responsible for whatever merit I possess. Vanity is simply a silly preoccupation with God's lesser natural gifts, such as looks or talents.

It would not be humility — it would be a belittling of God's wisdom and goodness — to pretend that I do not amount to much, that my life is meaningless, that I would never have been missed if I had not been born. It is quite true that apart from God I am nothing. It is just as true that God's love has made me great. To admit this is to do simple justice to God. I must never surrender to the temptation to think, "I am no good. I am a failure."

Neither must I surrender — ever — to self-pity; to the feeling that nobody loves me, nobody cares about me. How awful it would be, after all the love God has expended and is expending on me, to brood and sorrow because I do not receive as much human love as I might wish. That would be about as silly as the complaint of a millionaire at not winning on the penny slot machine. A self-pitying person can only be one who is weak in faith or ignorant in religion. God's love for me is such a tremendous thing!

From my sense of Christian vocation there follows another effect: freedom from serious worry. If I really believe that God loves me with an infinite love (as He does) and that He wants what is best for me (as He does), I cannot worry very long or very intensely. God is infinitely wise; He always knows what is best. God is infinitely powerful; He can accomplish anything He wishes. So how can I go wrong, how can I lose, as long as I try to do my best with such talents and knowledge as God has given me?

✤

God can bring good out of your mistakes

I shall make mistakes, of course, not being infallible. Yet, out of my very mistakes God will bring good, and my very stupidity God will in some way turn to my account. The father who backs his car out of the garage and runs over his own child; the mother who overexerts herself and loses her baby: such persons cannot, of course, escape their natural sorrow at the thought of what might have been. However, they would be wanting in faith if they let themselves go through life guilt-ridden and remorseful. They would be wanting in faith if they did not feel confident that out of their human errors God would, in some way, bring good.

I must see this, too, in the miseries that come to me and others through the malice of my fellow humans. God has endowed us with free wills in order that we may be capable of loving Him. Without freedom there can be no love; love must be freely given, or it is not love at all. Yet, freedom is a dangerous gift. It can be, and often is, abused. As a consequence, innocent persons sometimes suffer because of the evil will of another. Thoughtlessly we may say, "Why does God let them do it?" We forget that if God were to destroy every person who was on the verge of causing unhappiness to another, you and I might have been eliminated long ago.

The pertinent point is that the evil which men do does not defeat God's purposes. He simply fits the evil into His plan and bends it to His will. The hatred of the Pharisees for Christ became the tool of our own redemption. The cruelty of Roman emperors peopled Heaven with glorious martyrs and speeded the growth of the Church. Out of the tyranny of Communism may well come a new Christian civilization. Coming down to my own level, that unkind deed that was done to me yesterday will end in profit, not loss, to me; of that I am sure.

I cannot exaggerate God's love for me, God's care for me. He loves me a hundred times, a thousand times more than I love myself. I am never out of His mind or His attention. And it is not my happiness only in the next life that interests God — that most of all, of course. But, just as Jesus had compassion on the hungry multitude and worked a miracle to feed them,[2] so, too, is God concerned with my happiness here and now. Being human, I cannot escape suffering or dismiss worry completely. But, understanding God's urgent love for me, His concern for me, I will never be crushed by suffering or defeated by worry.

God loves me. His love enfolds me — let us dare to say it — in a hungry embrace. If I lose God, it will be because I have willfully rejected Him, never because He has cast me off. God loves me. This is the whole reason for my existence. Upon my understanding and grasp of this fact my whole spiritual life must be built.

[2] Cf. Matt. 14:14-21.

Chapter Three

✂

See sin for what it is

❧

Whenever I speak of sin — particularly, mortal sin — there comes to my mind the grim memory of a tragedy I once witnessed. A child of three was running across the lawn of his home, pursued by his mother. "Come back, Timmy, come back!" she was calling, "Don't go into the street!" But Timmy, reveling in his escape from the backyard fence, had no ears for her. He scooted happily between the automobiles parked at the curb, and a passing car tossed his broken body almost into his mother's arms.

Except that Timmy was too young to be responsible for his actions, this is a picture of God and the sinner. "Come back, come back!" God cries out anxiously with His grace as the soul moves toward sin. But the sinner, oblivious to everything except his own desire, shuts out God's voice and goes willfully to his death.

❧

Sin involves stupidity

Stupidity is an element that figures prominently in sin. A sin, we know, is a deliberate act of disobedience to God. When we sin, we either do something God has forbidden or we refuse to do something God has commanded. We choose to forget or we ignore the fact that God has given us His commandments for our own benefit, not for His. His commandments are the "backyard fence" that God has built for us to preserve us from hurting ourselves and others.

To appreciate this fact, we have only to imagine what the world would be like if everyone kept God's commandments. There would be no crime, no injustice, no cruelty, no dishonesty, no illegitimate births, and no broken homes. There would be no police, no prisons, no armies or navies. All men would live in complete peace and harmony with one another. Admittedly this is a utopia that will never come about. There will always be humans who listen to the voice of their own particular serpent in their own Eden — to the voice of their own pride or lust or avarice.

However, even though much of the world may reject God's recipe for happiness, each individual can still find, through the observance of God's laws, the highest degree of happiness that this life can afford. It is this fact, the fact that he is sabotaging his own happiness, that the sinner stupidly refuses to see.

If we buy an expensive piece of equipment, whether it be a washer, a movie camera, or a stereo, we are very careful to follow the directions the manufacturer has provided. We realize that the maker knows best how the machine should be handled for greatest effectiveness and with least damage.

God is our Maker. Surely He knows best the way in which we should use ourselves. In His commandments He has given us the "book of directions," which will enable us to obtain the fullest degree of happiness from life. What folly it is for any one of us to think that he knows, better than God, the direction in which happiness lies — to think that he is smarter than God. Yet this is the crooked reasoning behind all sin. "I want to do it. I know that God says I mustn't. But in this case, I know better than God what is best for me. God or no God, I'm going to do what I want." We sadly remark on the stupidity of a motorist who, hurrying to keep a golfing date, ignores the traffic laws and crashes to his death as he tries to pass another car on a curve. Even more stupid is the sinner who ignores God's commandments and rushes to an even greater ruin.

The harm a sinner does himself is not only graver than physical death; it also is less obvious. Perhaps a better example than the motorist would be the example of a man who would ignore the warnings of radiologists and would handle radioactive materials without proper shielding. Here, as in sin, the damage is not at once apparent. The destruction of his health is deep and deadly, although on the surface nothing seems to have changed. Similarly, the sinner may feel that he has "gotten away with it." He seems to be safe in the enjoyment of his disobedience. Yet inwardly the destruction of his real happiness has been wrought. In his stubborn pride he may refuse to admit it, but the sinner discovers, perhaps too late, that God's directions would have worked best after all.

Sin involves ingratitude

Besides the element of stupidity in sin, there is also the element of gross ingratitude. God made me because, for some reason unfathomable to me, He loved the very thought of me in His divine mind. From all eternity He has cherished that thought of me and has desired to share with me forever His own inexpressible happiness. At a certain point in time He created me, and ever since then He has offered me innumerable helps and graces. He even went to such lengths as to become a human being like me and to die on a Cross in order to provide me with those graces. (Here I need to remind myself again that Jesus would have died for me even if I had been the only soul on earth in need of salvation.)

God has done everything that even His infinite wisdom can devise in order to bring me to the happiness He wants me to have. There is just one thing that God cannot do for me. There is just one part of the plan that only I can perform: I must love God. It is my love for God that makes me capable of the happiness of Heaven. Without love for God in my heart, I am no more capable of enjoying the happiness of Heaven than a piece of glass is capable of conducting electricity. Even God, for all His infinite power, cannot impart His happiness to me if I have not prepared myself for it by loving Him. Without love for God, Heaven would mean less to me than a symphony would mean to a cow. God will *help* me to love Him. Indeed, without His grace I would be incapable of loving Him. But the act of my free will by which I choose God above and beyond all others as my supreme good — this act I must make, and no one else can make it for me.

My love for God is not a matter of sentiment. Even in human love, emotion is an undependable yardstick. A man may cry in his beer as he listens to a tenor sing "Mother Machree" and still continue to break his mother's heart by his rascality. It is by what we do for a person, the sacrifices we are willing to make for a person, that we truly prove our love, not by how we feel toward the person. This is even truer of our love for God. Our love for Him is rooted in our will, not in our emotions. If we are willing to do for God anything He asks, then we do love Him — but only then.

God gave us His commandments for our own good and not primarily as tests of our love. Nevertheless they do become the instruments by which we prove our love. If I love God, I will do what God asks me to do, no matter what sacrifice I have to make of my own preferences. Either I obey Him, or I do not love Him. There is no middle course.

It is here that the black ingratitude of sin becomes visible. To use a slang phrase, God has "knocked Himself out" to show His love for me and to confer happiness upon me — especially the supreme happiness of union with Him in Heaven. All this God has done, and I, in my sin, thumb my nose at Him. Loving myself more than Him, I refuse to take the one step, the step of obedience, that would complete God's efforts. I *will* have this moment of self-satisfaction, this physical pleasure, this monetary gain, this satisfying revenge. If it means rejecting God and His love — well, that's just too bad for God. This is what my sinful action says.

⁂

We make excuses for our sins

Of course, I cannot face the full implications of my action and still continue to sin. I dare not admit, even to myself, that

I do not love God. So I refuse to listen to the voice of conscience. I resolutely keep my mind off the stupidity and the ingratitude of what I am doing, so that afterward I can say to myself, "I didn't really mean to do wrong." Yet, pretending that the evil isn't there will not make it go away. I cannot so easily escape the consequences of my sin.

Another defensive device is to pretend to myself that in this particular case, under these special circumstances, God's law doesn't apply to me. This is the reasoning, for example, of the man who marries a divorced woman. "My children need a mother," he will say. "Besides, I love her. God will understand." Such reasoning seems to envision God as a child-spoiling granny who indulgently looks the other way while little Roscoe stuffs himself with forbidden sweets. But we cannot change God's nature by our pretending. We cannot make Him to be what, for this moment, we would like Him to be. God is not a senile, indulgent, "tut-tut, poor child" sort of nursemaid. Pretend as I may, His justice endures.

Still another way to alibi for sin is to make an imaginary distinction between God and His Church, the Church that He died to establish. The technique here is to pretend that we are willing to obey God's laws, provided that we are satisfied (by some standard of our own) that they really are God's laws. We insist on being the judge of that. Or, to put it another way, we will obey a command that comes to us personally from God, but not any obligation that seems to come to us secondhand.

I recall here a woman who boasted to her bridge club that, although she received the sacraments regularly, she would never tell in Confession of her use of contraceptives. "The Church is too strict about that," she maintained, "and it isn't any of the priest's business." We can imagine Jesus (who said to His Church, "He who hears you hears me"[3]) twisting in renewed agony on the Cross at such distorted reasoning.

The truth is that the Church is Christ's own Mystical Body. Christ lives in His Church. We cannot drive a wedge between Christ and His own Body. Our faith is already well on the way to dying if we say, "It is only a law of the Church."

Actually, loss of faith *is* a frequent result of long-continued sin. We cannot bear to live in constant conflict with ourselves. We cannot sustain for long a war within us. If our faith continues to chide us for some behavior we refuse to abandon, we must make some kind of peace for ourselves, however unreal the peace may be. Something must give; if not our behavior, then our faith. So we begin to suspect that our faith is untrue.

This, then, is the story of sin. It is a story of stupidity and of ingratitude; a story of genuine happiness exchanged for phony pleasure; a story of love extinguished and faith lost. We have need, all of us, to pray daily, "O Jesus, save me from sin!"

[3] Luke 10:16.

Chapter Four

&

Avoid serious sin

❧

A man once asked me, "Father, how can I keep from mortal sin?" I reminded the gentleman that he had learned the answer to that question years ago in his catechism. Be faithful to daily prayer, and pray especially in times of temptation. Receive the sacraments frequently. Avoid the persons and places and things that might lead you into sin.

"I haven't forgotten that," he answered, "and I try to do all those things. But for me it doesn't seem to be enough."

"Then perhaps you have forgotten what it takes to make a mortal sin," I said. "Perhaps you think you are committing mortal sin when really you are not. To a person who really is doing his best, God *always* gives enough grace to keep him from mortal sin."

In the fulfillment of our duty to love God, the avoidance of mortal sin is the first and most essential step. Mortal sin and love for God are exact opposites. Mortal sin by its very nature involves a rejection of God, a denial of love to God. The disobedience exhibited in venial sin differs not only in degree, but also in kind, from the disobedience that marks mortal sin.

An example from family life may help to illustrate this difference. Mother and Dad, going out to work in the garden, tell Sally to do the supper dishes. Sally doesn't want to miss her favorite TV program, so she neglects the dishes. When they come in, Mother and Dad are understandably annoyed, but they are not hurt. They know that there was no real malice in Sally's disobedience.

On the other hand, one night Molly stands defiantly in the front door. "Don't try to tell me when to come home," she shouts at her parents. "I'll come home when I please, and you can like it or lump it." And she slams the door. Here we have disobedience with real malice, disobedience that includes rejection of the parents and contempt for their authority.

Between the disobedience of Sally and that of Molly, there is a difference of *kind*, not merely of degree. Similarly there is a difference, from God's viewpoint, between venial and mortal sin — a difference that is immeasurable.

There are three prerequisites of mortal sin

The avoidance of mortal sin is absolutely essential to the practice of the love of God. It also is the primary proof that we love God. It is highly important, then, that we have a clear understanding of the elements that constitute a mortal sin. It would be a most unhappy mistake for us to think that we are committing mortal sin if really we are not. For a sin to be mortal, we recall that the three requisites are: that the thing we do (or the duty we omit) is a serious matter, that we have a sufficient understanding of what we are doing, and that we fully consent to our action. Each of these three deserves close examination.

A *serious matter* means that it is serious from God's viewpoint, regardless of how men may esteem it. There are persons who will admit that adultery is a grave matter, but who hold that "a bit of petting" is of little consequence. To God, both are grave matters. Some will admit that murder is a major evil, yet will easily condone an abortion. To God, both are damnable. Some will condemn robbery at the point of a gun, but will think little of defrauding another in a business deal. In God's eyes, there is little to choose between the two.

In assessing the gravity of sin in our own lives, we have to be very sure that we keep our thinking in line with God's. It would be a great mistake for us to exaggerate the gravity of a matter; to think, for example, that we have committed a mortal sin because we have used God's name in vain or have told a simple lie. However, when the matter is serious, it is a favorite stratagem of the Devil (or perhaps of our own self-love) to whisper, "This thing has been greatly overrated. It can't really be as bad as all that!"

Sufficient understanding means that I know what I am doing and am aware that what I am doing is a sin. It is obvious that no one could commit a sin in his sleep, no matter what crime he might perpetrate in his dreams. It is equally obvious that a person could not commit a sin through simple forgetfulness — for example, by missing Mass because he has forgotten that it is a holy day of obligation. Neither can a person commit sin through error or ignorance, unless the error or ignorance is his own fault. I should not feel guilty today if I discover that something I did yesterday is really a sin, although I did not know it at the time. Adults sometimes torture themselves needlessly with guilt feelings concerning some childhood action, the gravity of which they did not even realize when it happened.

Of course, this matter of sufficient understanding works both ways. If I deliberately do something, thinking it is a sin, then it *is* a sin for me — even though I later find out that my action was permissible. If I steal some money and later find out that it was my own money that I took, I have still sinned. I willed to offend God, and my ignorance cannot destroy the malice of that act of the will.

On this point of sufficient understanding, there is one subtle danger we have to guard against. This is the danger of deliberately blinding ourselves to the possibility of sin. We can slyly walk toward sin or let ourselves be led willingly toward it, all the while pretending to ourselves that we do not recognize the danger. Afterward, our defense is that we were taken by surprise, but it is not a defense that will deceive God.

Full consent of the will is needed for the rejection of God that constitutes mortal sin. This means that what we do, we do deliberately. We are not capable of the freedom of decision necessary for a mortal sin if some factor seriously interferes with our liberty of choice. It is plain that if we are physically forced to do something, it could not be a sin for us. But there are other factors that may destroy or lessen our freedom of will. We could be influenced by grave fear, or severe anxiety, or extreme fatigue, or by nervous tension, or by a hidden emotional conflict. Depending on the degree to which our ability to decide may be influenced, sin that is by its nature mortal might become for us a venial sin or no sin at all.

It is perhaps in this area of freedom that the malice of mortal sin most often is reduced to venial proportions. There are obscure influences at work in all of us. An unhappy childhood may have left lasting marks. We may suffer from feelings of rejection, inferiority, failure, or lack of personal worth. Only God can know the effect of such deep-seated influences on our power of rational and deliberate decision. Often, only God can know the degree of free consent that a person has given to an action. Only God can know the gravity of the sin.

Frequently, too, it is only God who can know whether we have said no to a temptation quickly enough. This is likely to be true, especially, with respect to sinful thoughts. A sinful thought may come into my mind, perhaps against charity, or against faith, or against chastity. The thought may linger for some moments. Then I realize that it is a sinful thought and eventually try to put it out of my mind. The thought may come back again and again, stubbornly refusing to be so easily dismissed. Afterward, I wonder, "Did I try to dismiss the thought soon enough? Did I willingly accept it and let it linger in my mind to the point of sin?"

Often we cannot answer the question ourselves. We have to be content to make an act of contrition and leave the answer to God. It is almost certain, however, that we have *not* sinned grievously if, day by day, we honestly are trying to keep from mortal sin. The doubt is in our favor.

There is one point, touching the deliberate choice of sin, that sometimes is overlooked. This is the fact that the malice of sin lies in the intention rather than in the action. The moment I deliberately make up my mind to commit a certain sin, I have already committed that sin as far as God is concerned. For example, suppose I make up my mind to steal a hundred dollars. In that moment, I commit the sin. Perhaps when I go to get the hundred dollars, it is no longer there, or perhaps I change my mind and decide not to steal it after all. I still have been guilty of a grave sin. Changing my mind afterward cannot wipe out a sin that already has been committed.

It may be said (as I have heard it said), "Then I might as well go ahead and take the money anyway, as long as the sin has already been committed." Aside from the sophistry of saying, "I might as well keep on sinning, once I've started," or, "Why repent now?" there is the further fact that the outward act adds malice to the inner act. This is particularly true when my outward action violates the rights of another person.

⚭

Take care to stay free
from mortal sin

With the grace that God will give, we all can always keep from mortal sin. This is a truth of faith. No matter how strong our temptations may be, God's grace always will be stronger. There will never be a time when I can commit a mortal sin and truthfully say afterward, "I couldn't help it." If I really and truly couldn't help it, then of course it wasn't a mortal sin at all. If what I mean is that I could not help it at the time it happened because I neglected the due precautions against sin, then of course the sin is still mine.

If I have strong temptations, yet skimp on my daily prayers and fail to pray in time of temptation, then it is little wonder if I sin. If I neglect regular Confession and frequent Holy Communion, sin should come as no surprise. It was to provide the strength we ourselves lack that Jesus gave us these sacraments. If I neglect Confession and Holy Communion, I am saying, in effect, "I don't care much whether I sin. I'll take my chances with temptation."

Even more foolhardy is the person who makes no effort to avoid the occasion of sin or perhaps even seeks the occasion of sin. Examples would be the young couple who park in lovers' lane; the man who goes to a strip-tease performance; the woman who reads the latest obscene best-seller; the girl (or man) who dates a divorced person.

With prayer, the sacraments, and the avoidance of unnecessary danger, we can — and surely we do — keep free from mortal sin. God asks only that we do our honest best. If we are doing that best, we can lay to rest any doubts or scruples that may afflict us.

Chapter Five

Avoid even venial sin

✂

We do not stop growing at the age of eighteen or twenty-one. We stop growing physically, yes. But, unless we are mentally ill or senile, there is an urge within us that impels us to keep on growing in mind and in skills. If we did not want to grow mentally, there would not be such an expanding market for books and periodicals of all kinds. We always are seeking to increase our knowledge of people, of events, and of the world around us.

We desire, too, to perfect our skills. No matter how good a cook you may be, it is very likely that you still collect recipes, try new dishes, and read the kitchen page of your favorite magazine. If you play bridge, however expertly, you still hold postmortems to examine how you might have played this hand or that one better. If you are a golfer, even with a low handicap, you keep trying to perfect your grip, your stance, or your swing. Even if you are a successful parent, a lecture or an article on how to raise children still will get your close attention. So it goes, through the whole gamut of human activity. Whether you swim, skate, bowl, garden, run a business, or practice medicine, you always seek to do it a little better.

That is, almost always. There is one department of life — the most important department — in which people are content with mediocrity. This is the realm of the spiritual. Improvement here will pay everlasting dividends. Yet, without putting it into words, we all too often assume, "I'm good enough." Theoretically we agree with the fact that no one actually is "good enough" from God's standpoint. No one ever is as good as God wills him to be. Yet we somehow manage to agree with the theory without letting it disturb the comfortable spiritual groove into which we have settled.

Our one overall obligation in life is to love God. The minimum requisite in the fulfillment of this duty is that we obey God in the things that matter most to Him. The primary and absolutely essential expression of our love consists in the avoidance of mortal sin. The "I don't care what God wants" spirit of mortal sin is the very antithesis of love for God. It can be assumed that we do try, and try resolutely, to keep from mortal sin.

In the practice of the love of God, the next step upward is the firm renunciation of all deliberate venial sin. Here again, most people would probably say, if asked, "No, of course I would not deliberately offend God, even in a small matter." Yet, in many instances, our defense against deliberate venial sin will be found to be weak and ineffective.

Perhaps the term *deliberate venial sin* calls for examination. We recognize that there is no such thing as a completely indeliberate venial sin. An action that is wholly unintentional could not be a sin at all. Conceivably we could transgress God's law through complete forgetfulness, or through unavoidable ignorance, or through accident, or in sleep. Such actions are totally lacking in malice and are sinless.

However, there are venial sins that are semideliberate. These are sins committed without full purposefulness. They might happen through sudden surprise, or carelessness, or lack of full attention to what we are doing for one reason or another. An example is the man who drops a brick on his toes and bursts into profanity. He isn't wholly unconscious of the fact that his language is offensive to God, yet the pain of the moment robs his words of deliberate malice. Another example is the dog-tired mother who becomes irrationally angry over a bit of spilled milk. Her fatigue greatly diminishes the willfulness of her temper tantrum. Still another example is the husband who, asked by his wife whether he mailed her letter, gives a quick yes as he remembers that the letter is still in his pocket. In his sudden consternation, he only half-adverts to the fact that he is telling a lie.

These would be classified as semideliberate venial sins. There is a notable difference between them and such premeditated acts as stealing an ashtray or a towel from the hotel where we have stayed; carefully thinking up a lie in advance in order to explain our absence from work; or passing along a choice bit of gossip, not gravely harmful, about my neighbor. In these cases, I know full well what I am doing, and my venial sin is deliberate.

One of the saddest phrases on the lips of man are the words "It's only a venial sin." With these words I convict myself of possessing a low-grade love for God. In things that mean a lot to Him, I will obey, but I won't go quite all the way with Him.

Certainly parents would feel sore at heart over a child who would say, "I'll obey Mom and Dad in the big things, but I'll do as I please in the little things." Parents would grieve over the weakness of such love — and we are God's children.

We know that no number of venial sins will add up to a mortal sin. There is a limitless difference between the total rejection of God involved in mortal sin and the petty selfishness toward God exhibited in venial sin. However, repeated venial sin does progressively cool the ardor of our love for God. Like corrosion inside a water pipe, it lessens the capacity of our soul to contain God's grace. In other words, venial sin weakens us spiritually. Just as lesser illnesses can make the body more susceptible to serious contagion, so does deliberate and habitual venial sin make easier our surrender to mortal sin.

⁂

Venial sin isn't worth the
pleasure it may bring

Moreover, from a purely practical standpoint, venial sin cannot possibly pay. When we commit venial sin, we usually do so for some small personal advantage. We tell a lie to save ourselves a momentary embarrassment. We steal some stamps from the boss's desk to save a few pennies. We make a catty remark about someone to get even for what she said about us. We take that one-drink-too-many to escape our anxieties or our self-consciousness. We use profanity toward an employee to let him know we mean business. We get to Sunday Mass a little late so that we can be first out of the parking lot. And so it goes.

Avoid even venial sin

Apparently, we forget we are dealing with God. He has the world and all things in it in the palm of His hand. Can we suppose that He will encourage us in our disobedience by allowing us to profit from our "little sins"? He has His own ways of evening the score. I avoid a little embarrassment by my lie today, only to face a bigger and inescapable embarrassment tomorrow. I save pennies by stealing stamps only to find tomorrow that I have to buy a new tire. I salve my pride today with my catty remark and tomorrow encounter a grave humiliation. I drown my worries with that excess drink and am faced with a new and bigger worry tomorrow. I cuss out an employee and find later that someone else has got a chunk of business that I had hoped for. I get away first from the parking lot, then find that I have to lose two hours repairing a leaky water pipe.

God's penalties are not always so obvious. Nevertheless, we are fools to think we can gain by venial sin. If it were a matter of mortal sin, God's justice might wait for the next world. But venial sin, we can count on it, will be balanced here and now. Not completely, perhaps: there may still be Purgatory. Yet God, in His love for us, will try to teach us our lesson.

Then there is the matter of making an act of perfect contrition. We all hope to be able to make an act of perfect contrition whenever the danger of death may face us. We know that an act of perfect contrition will take away all mortal sin from the soul and will prepare us for a happy judgment. We frequently try to make acts of perfect contrition now, so that we may be able to do so in time of emergency.

However, an act of perfect contrition means that we are sorry for our sins mainly out of love for God, not because we are afraid of losing Heaven and incurring Hell. This kind of sorrow will not come easily to a person who is unwilling to renounce all deliberate venial sin. Love for God is very weak in a person who is prepared to commit a venial sin any time he deems it useful.

Moreover, unless we have set our will firmly against deliberate venial sin, we cannot gain a plenary indulgence for ourselves. A plenary indulgence is a complete wiping out of any debt we may owe to God. If we were to die immediately after gaining a plenary indulgence, we would enter Heaven at once. However, one of the conditions for gaining a plenary indulgence is that we have true sorrow, not only for all mortal sins, but also for all deliberate venial sins. There can be no true sorrow without a purpose of amendment. Hence, to gain a plenary indulgence, we must have our will solidly set against all deliberate venial sin.

Venial sin just isn't worth it. From every point of view, it just isn't worth the price we have to pay for it. It is to be hoped, however, that in our evaluation of venial sin, all other considerations will be secondary to our love for God. We have taken a long step forward, we have achieved real spiritual growth, if we can sincerely pray, "I want to love You, God, with all my heart and soul. I do not want to measure out my love for You in dribs and drabs. I will not be content with the minimum. I will not stop at avoiding mortal sin only. *All* sin that is deliberate I renounce. Help me, dear God, to grow daily in fidelity, in things little as well as big. Help me to grow in love for You!"

Chapter Six

❦

Be prepared for God's judgment

⚛

No two deaths are alike, as any parish priest can testify. Looking back through the thirty-three years of my own ministry, a great variety of deathbed scenes throng to the forefront of memory.

There is the eighty-year-old nun, calm and unafraid as she receives Holy Viaticum.[4] Not only is she unafraid; she is even eager for the moment when she will look upon the face of the Master whom she has loved and served so well through all her years. The pleasures she gave up, the sacrifices she made, the humble and hidden life she led — these she counts as nothing now. Her soul almost visibly strains at the leash to go to God. She smiles as I turn to leave the room. "Goodbye, Father," she whispers. "Please pray that He may come soon."

Another recollection is that of the mother who has worried, through her long and painful illness, about the husband and half-grown children she will leave behind. She has been a good wife and mother. Through her prayers and example, her

---

[4] Viaticum ("provision for the journey") is Holy Communion that is given to the dying.

children have learned the real meaning of love for God, and her husband, too, has grown in spiritual stature. Now the grace of confidence has come to her, as it so often does at the end. The crease of worry has left her forehead. Her voice is faint but serene as she tells me, "God will be mother to my children now, Father. I know He wouldn't take me without making it up to them a hundred times over. And in Heaven I can do ever so much more for them than I ever could do here on earth."

Yet another scene comes to me. I am anointing the still-warm body of a middle-aged man who, just a few minutes ago, slumped dead at his desk of a heart attack. Even as I speak the prayers of conditional anointing, I remember that he spent an hour last Saturday night at nocturnal adoration. I remember, too, that this very morning I gave Holy Communion to him and his wife at the seven o'clock Mass, as I have done almost every morning these past several years. His death was sudden, but far from unprovided for. I can almost hear God saying, "Come, my son. The last sacraments are for those who need them. As for you, just come quickly!"

Some of the greatest consolations of a priest's life are the happy deathbeds at which he assists. There is always the human sorrow to contend with, the sorrow of the living at this separation from one whom they have loved. But this human sorrow cannot dampen the greater joy of seeing a good soul go to God.

Unfortunately, there is another side to the picture. Not all scenes of death are a source of spiritual joy. There is one type of deathbed I always leave with an uneasy heart. This is the deathbed of a person who for a long time has flouted God's

love and made a mockery of God's grace. He or she has neglected prayer, the Mass, and the sacraments, possibly for
years. He has lived in a state of habitual sin, complacent in his
self-love and with no thought of a final accounting. Now he
knows he is going to die, and he fears with a great fear. He
makes his confession, and he renounces his sins with violent
emphasis. He receives the Anointing of the Sick and Holy
Viaticum. Yet there is a distasteful question in the priest's
mind as he completes his ministrations: "Does this person
have real sorrow for his sins, or is he just frightened?" The answer is known only to God.

It is true that fear of the Lord is a wholesome thing — but
not craven, servile fear; not the fear of a dog cringing under
the master's whip. Our fear of God must be the reverential fear
that a child has of his parents. This is a fear compounded of
respect, dependency, and some beginning of love. It is not a
fear of naked punishment, but a fear of losing the approval of
someone whose approval we highly value. Every parent sees
this kind of fear in constant operation. The child cries, not
because the slight slap has pained him, but because the slap
expresses his parent's displeasure. It is reverential fear that
makes the parent's displeasure hurt more than the slap.

There are persons who live lives of religious neglect, indif-
ferent to God's rights and to His commandments. In the back
of such a person's mind there may be a half-formed intention:
"I'll start being good when I get old," or, "I'll repent before I
die." Such a person seems unaware that true repentance for sin
is a grace of God. Without God's grace, we cannot make a genuine act of contrition. The habitual sinner dares God to refuse

that grace when he, the sinner, is ready for it. This is to presume on God's mercy, and so the sinner adds the sin of daily
presumption to his other offenses.

It is the deathbed of such a person that leaves a priest's
heart sad and questioning. "Is he really sorry? Or, knowing
that he faces judgment and Hell, is he only scared?" Even in
Confession, our sorrow for sin must be a supernatural sorrow,
and this is not a grace to be conjured up at will. One reason
the priest is dubious about some deathbed repentances is that
he has seen instances in which the penitent has recovered
and has soon returned to his life of easy sin. Only God can
read a heart, but it seems doubtful that that person's purpose of
amendment could have been real.

⚬

Be ready for death

The most important moment of our lives is the moment of
our death. In that moment we are fixed forever in the mold in
which death finds us. When I was a child and would pout or
grimace, my mother would say, "Look out, or that face will
freeze on you!" Although I knew she was joking, the thought
of such a fate was enough to clear the distortion from my face.
God is not joking, however, when He tells us that as we live, so
shall we die. Death will "freeze" forever our spiritual condition
of that moment: our state of grace or our state of mortal sin.
On that single split second of our passing hangs our eternal
union with God or our eternal separation from Him.

Perhaps you have watched the showing of amateur movies
in some friend's home. In a jocose mood, the friend suddenly

flicked the switch and stopped the projector. There on the screen a face was caught and suspended in action: perhaps a silly simper, a squinting frown, or a flashing smile. It was funny, and everyone laughed. However, it will be no laughing matter when death presses the switch and our soul is caught and held forever in its beauty or its ugliness.

Then "after death, the judgment."[5] The thought of this ordeal is enough to cause some qualms even in the best of us. What will it be like to face Absolute Truth, with no chance to dodge or evade, no hope of excusing ourselves or of pretending that it isn't so?

In this life, it is almost impossible to be absolutely honest with ourselves. We strain to give ourselves the benefit of every doubt. Even to ourselves we put the best possible interpretation on our faults and failures. "Anyone would have done what I did if they had been in my place" is a universal favorite. But in our judgment after death, there will not be an "anyone" to whom I can point for justification. "You don't expect me to be a saint, do you?" is another favorite. At our judgment, God's answer will be "Yes, that is precisely what I expected." Still another overworked alibi is "After all, I'm only human." God's answer will be "Yes, but the grace I gave you was divine."

God's judgment will reveal who you really are
No one knows exactly what the particular judgment will be like, except that it will be immediate and final. The instant

---

[5] Cf. Heb. 9:27.

the soul leaves the body, it will be judged. In that same instant, the soul will begin its eternity of Heaven (with a possible stopover in Purgatory) or of Hell. Very likely, say theologians, our soul will simply be illuminated in the searching light of God's infinite justice. We shall be exposed to Truth, like a lone actor pinpointed by a spotlight in the middle of an empty stage, with every wrinkle and bit of grease paint in merciless clarity.

In a sense, each of us will be his own judge. In that instant of divine illumination, we shall see every grace we ever have received and every sin we have ever committed. We shall see every opportunity we have wasted, every hurt we have done to another, and every person we were intended to help but did not. We shall see, too, the consequences of all our actions down through the reaches of eternity. This will be a fateful time for parents who have neglected the spiritual training of their children — and for all of us who have given scandal to others.

To our comfort, however, we should remember that it is a moment of divine truth. Consequently, we shall also see every least good deed we have performed, every smallest sacrifice we have made for God; and each shall shine with blazing glory. Along with the wrinkles and the scars, we shall see also the extenuating factors that may have lessened our responsibility: the influences of our environment, the neglect (if any) we suffered from our own parents, the pressures of emotional stress and mental strain. Like data fed into a computer, all elements will combine in that one great moment of self-revelation. For the first time we shall see ourselves, totally, as we really are.

Be prepared for God's judgment

The answer will come out in simple terms: either we love God, or we do not.

⁂

Meditate on death

It is good for us, from time to time, to meditate on death — even to visualize the moment of our own death. At our beside there will be the sound of sobbing. Someone will gently close our eyes and fold our hands. Yet, even before the sheet has been drawn over our now-still face, we shall have stood under God's revealing light. We shall have been judged. The prayers for the dying may still be echoing in the room, but our eternity will have begun.

We must realize that death and judgment are facts, not fantasy. The description given here may be inadequate, but with absolute certainty it is going to happen to you! What fools we are if we do not live with an eye to this tremendous moment. It is the moment for which God made us, the moment toward which our whole life is directed. And we are rushing toward it so fast — like a river toward its waterfall!

Chapter Seven

Let the thought of Heaven inspire you to be holy

❧

I remember the first Cinerama. The show began with a black-and-white movie on a screen of conventional size, with Lowell Thomas giving a brief lecture on the history of motion pictures. The lecture ended with the announcement "And *this* is Cinerama." At that moment, the curtains slid back from either side of the small screen, to expose a screen that filled the entire front of the theater. With explosive suddenness Cinerama began, to the sound of screams and clicking rails and rushing air. The whole theater was on a roller coaster, rushing down the grades, banking on the turns. I leaned sideways in my seat and could feel the pressure on my bottom as we roared around the curves. I still can recall the thrill of that sudden transition from a quiet lecture in a movie of old-time size, to the stomach-churning ride on the huge Cinerama screen.

The example is ridiculously weak, but I can think of nothing that better illustrates what will happen to the person who dies free from all sin. He has found this world attractive only because he has never known a better world. Then he closes his eyes on this world, and opens them on his new world — which is God Himself.

The bursting excitement of that moment, the soul-vibrating happiness of that moment, is something no one can imagine or describe. Even a saint from Heaven would have to give up in despair to describe it to us. St. Paul was given, in a vision, a foretaste of Heaven. All that he could say of it afterward was "Eye has not seen, nor ear heard, nor has it entered into the heart of man, what things God has prepared for those who love Him."[6]

However, we can and do try to get some faint idea of what the happiness of Heaven will be like.

If we have been fortunate enough to experience some major happiness in life, we can begin with that as an example. We can look back to that moment of exquisite happiness, whenever and whatever it was. A married couple might look back to the day of their marriage; a nun might look back to the day of her religious profession, a priest to the day of his ordination. Whatever was the moment of that memorable happiness, we can multiply it in imagination by a thousand million. We will still fall short in our comprehension of the happiness of Heaven.

Even by great leaps of the imagination, it is hard to conceive what it will be like to look upon God. He is infinitely lovable. This means that He will be irresistible. The very sight of Him will siphon love out of us as the heart of a tornado sucks the water from a lake over which it passes. Up from our very roots, up from our figurative toes, love will rush out of us to God.

[6] 1 Cor. 2:9.

Let the thought of Heaven inspire you

⚘

In Heaven, you will love and be lovable

From time to time, a publicity agent will dub a certain actor or actress "the Great Lover." In Heaven we shall be astonished to find that each of us is a Great Lover. At present we are like birds raised in a cage, who have no idea of their capacity for soaring through the skies. Similarly, we have no idea of our capacity for loving. There is no human being who is capable of calling forth our total capacity for loving, of completely exhausting our power to love. God, however, is precisely such a Being. To use the only term that seems to fit, we shall *explode* with love as we look upon Him who is infinitely good, infinitely lovable.

To enjoy unalloyed happiness, it is not enough to love. We also must be certain that our love is returned. There will be no doubt of that, when God catches us up into His divine embrace.

God *is* love, infinite love. He made us because of His love for us. When the barrier of this earthly life is removed, God will be able to "let us have it with both barrels." The blast of His love will rock us and all but tear us apart. Right now, even the most prideful among us would not claim to be the most lovable person in all creation. Secretly we all recognize that we have some pretty unlovable spots. In Heaven, however, we shall find that we underrated ourselves while on earth. Cleansed from all sin and in the original beauty of soul with which God endowed us, we shall find that we are incredibly lovable. God will prove it to us as His love envelops us and carries us to dizzying heights of ecstasy.

65

⊰⊱

Heaven is eternal ecstasy

One further ingredient is needed to make our happiness complete. We must have certainty that this happiness will endure — this love at once so tender and so violent. Have you never exclaimed, in a moment of great happiness, "Oh, I wish that this could go on forever! I wish that it didn't have to end!" That is the final element in the happiness of Heaven: the fact that it is eternal.

Some earthbound minds become a little dubious at this point. They fear that even the happiness of Heaven may become monotonous and boring after a long time. Such minds fail to realize that the happiness of Heaven is not static happiness. It is not a "look at me while I look at you" sort of happiness. We have never been so active as we shall be in Heaven. God is *infinitely* lovable. This means that we never can exhaust His lovability. Through all eternity we shall be finding new facets, new depths of lovableness in God. Everlastingly we shall be turning corners, figuratively, and discovering in God new vistas of ecstatic excitement.

Another point to remember is that in Heaven there is no "long time." Time as we know it is strictly limited to the created universe. Eternity is not a long-drawn-out succession of hours and days. Eternity with God is just one splendid, razor-thin moment — but a moment that never ends.

Admittedly, we are banging our human minds against a ceiling when we try to visualize eternity. This is a concept that, like infinity, is wholly beyond our present comprehension. But let us attempt an illustration.

Let the thought of Heaven inspire you

Suppose that in Heaven you were to wear an eight-day watch, with each hour representing a billion years instead of sixty minutes. Now suppose that after your first quick look at God, you were able to take your eyes off Him long enough to flash a glance at your watch. You would find that your watch had run down.

This example (and indeed, all that I have said about Heaven) suffers from one great defect. It is too weak. It is inadequate to express the truth I am fumbling with. In speaking of God and of Heaven, there is never danger of exaggeration. The danger lies in the other direction. It is the danger that we may understand too poorly and value too lightly the nature of the happiness that God wants to give us.

✣

Your loved ones in Heaven will bring you joy

Thus far we have talked only of our relationship with God. Someone may ask, "But in Heaven, shall we also know and love those who were dear to us on earth?" In knowing God, we shall know all the souls God knows; in loving God, we shall necessarily love all the souls He loves. There will be an eternal interchange of love between God and other souls and ourselves — all of it one great and indivisible act of love, having its origin and its end in God. The interchange of love in Heaven will be like the circulation of blood in our bodies, which has its beginning and its terminus in the heart. In Heaven, God is the heart.

Yes, we shall be happy at the presence of our loved ones in Heaven. We shall have special cause for joy if they are there at least partly because of our prayers and good example; if we have had a share in presenting to God these souls who mean so much to Him.

But we have entirely missed the meaning of Heaven if we think of it as a place where we walk hand-in-hand with friends and family, listening to the music and swapping reminiscences. My own parents were very dear to me. I am confident that they are in Heaven and that I shall see them there — if, by God's mercy, I make it. But, speaking again in lame human terms, I do not see how either my parents or I will be able to tear our gaze from God long enough to have any real time or attention for each other. Whatever joy I may take in the presence of others in Heaven will be a very secondary joy. Whoever is or is not there, our own happiness will be total and undimmed — a happiness beyond our wildest dreams.

God gives you the graces you need to get to Heaven

And what chance is there that we may be able to enter into this happiness immediately after death? A very good chance, if we make a sustained effort to live day by day as God wants us to live. Surely this kind of loyalty gives us a claim upon God for whatever grace we may need in our last moments to die a completely happy death. This means to die, not only free from mortal sin, but free also from any venial sins or unpaid penance that might delay our entrance into Heaven. This, we know, is the principal purpose of the sacrament of Anointing of the Sick: to cleanse us from whatever "remains of sin" might impede our immediate flight to God.

Let the thought of Heaven inspire you

We may die suddenly, of course, with no opportunity for the holy anointing. For those who try to live according to God's will, this is no cause for grave concern. God's hands are not tied by the sacraments; He can give grace directly when He chooses. In our last moments, the mere mention in our heart of the name of Jesus, with love and with sorrow for sin, can be enough to bring us directly to God.

It is consoling to remember that God wants us in Heaven even more than we want to get there. If His grace can do it, He *will* get us there. And, once our time on earth is finished, God wants us in Heaven as quickly as possible. However, it would be folly for us to forget that God's mercy cannot eliminate His justice. Even He, in all His goodness, cannot force us into Heaven against our will. God's eager love cannot reach us if we have barred Him from our hearts by grave disobedience to His will.

If we have the least understanding of Heaven, we must see that it is worth living for, working for, and suffering for. We must see, too, that the only certain path to Heaven lies over the sometimes rugged but never impassable road of a good life. Surely we will agree that only a fool would gamble with such a heritage, even for a moment, by mortal sin.

Chapter Eight

⚬

Fear Hell

✌

"The worst thing about it was the awful loneliness. After a few months, I began to feel utterly abandoned and alone in the world. I felt that no one knew or cared where I was; that no one ever thought of me anymore." The speaker was a missionary who had suffered imprisonment at the hands of the Chinese Communists. For a year and a half, he had been kept in solitary confinement, not knowing what day might be his last. When he was finally released, his nerves were so shattered that, months later, he broke down and cried as he talked to me. He never has attempted again to describe the terrors of his long night, the depths of darkness in which his soul had been submerged.

His suffering is a good (although very faint) illustration of the suffering of Hell. I suppose that, to a certain extent, each of us sees Hell from some viewpoint of his own, in the light of whatever suffering he holds to be most acute. I once spent several days alone in a forest cabin. By the time some expected friends arrived, I could almost taste the loneliness like a bitterness in my mouth. Since then, in meditating on Hell, it is the black and absolute loneliness of Hell that disturbs me most.

One of the characteristics of Hell is a loneliness such as we never have conceived of. We are accustomed to saying that a person in Hell is a person who has died in the state of mortal sin. But, more basically, a person in Hell is a person who has refused God his love. Mortal sin is simply an acting out of this refusal. Completely cut off from God by his rejection of God, the sinner goes into eternity cut off from God forever. Separated from God, he is separated also from every soul that God has made. He finds himself in a vast, empty aloneness so utterly complete that it would be impossible to duplicate it on earth.

For one thing, if we are lonely in this life, we usually are buoyed up by the hope that something will happen to end our loneliness. Someone, surely, will come along, or our circumstances will change. In Hell this is not so. Death fixes us forever in the state in which it finds us. If we are without love for God when we die, there is no possibility of enkindling love for Him in our hearts after death. That is the horrible part of Hell: the consciousness, like a ceaseless chant in our ears that we cannot shut out: "This is forever, forever, forever."

Souls in Hell hate even themselves

Another essential difference between loneliness now and in Hell is that in this life we can, if we have to, live with ourselves. We may crave the companionship of others, but we can put up with our own company for a reasonable length of time. Indeed, in a busy life, we sometimes crave a chance just to be alone with ourselves. In Hell, however, there is a total lack of love. Without love for God, we love no one, not even ourselves.

Worse than that: a total lack of love is hatred. We have rejected God and, with Him, all else besides. We hate God, we hate our fellows, and we hate ourselves. This is the final refinement of the loneliness of Hell. Not merely have we condemned ourselves to an everlasting solitary existence; we are constrained, further, to live with a self we hate with a savage and immeasurable hatred. To the person in Hell, total extinction would be a million times better than life with himself. If he could, he gladly would tear his self to shreds and bits. His cry, if there were anyone to hear it, would be, "I hate God! I hate everyone! Most of all, I hate myself!"

This description of Hell as a great loneliness is a true description. It follows necessarily from the very nature of Hell as a state of eternal separation from God. But the loneliness, for all its horror, is a secondary kind of suffering. Our Lord Himself describes Hell as a fire that burns but does not consume and cannot be extinguished.[7] Jesus does not use words carelessly. Hence, we must see the essential pain of Hell as one of perpetual burning.

Souls in Hell search vainly for God

Our Lord does not define the nature of the fire of Hell. We know that it is not the kind of fire with which we are familiar here upon earth. For one thing, the fire we are familiar with

[7] Cf. Matt. 3:12.

consumes what it feeds upon. For another thing, the material fire of this world is incapable of hurting a spirit, of causing pain to a soul. Consequently, the nature of the fire of Hell has been the object of much speculation on the part of theologians.

One logical explanation is that hellfire is a burning that we inflict upon ourselves, by our eternally frustrated attempt to reach God. We are made for God, let us remember. In our soul there is a built-in attraction to God, like the attraction of a bit of iron to a magnet. In this life, we feel only faintly the straining of our soul toward God; perhaps we do not even recognize the urge for what it is. Our material body and human imperfection insulate us, to a great degree, against the drawing power of God. However, the instant death releases our soul from our body we shall feel the full force of God's pull upon us. If we die free from all sin, then death, judgment, and Heaven will be simultaneous. We shall go to God like a guided missile to its target.

If a person dies in the state of mortal sin, he will still experience this irresistible attraction of God for his soul. With all the power his spirit possesses, he will try to go to God. But he cannot. His own self-love has erected an impassable barrier. For all eternity, his effort to reach God continues, with a violence that never diminishes. It is all in vain. Without love for God, he cannot find God. There is no possible point of contact with God. And so he burns with the spiritual friction of trying to reach God and being eternally driven back upon himself. This, some theologians say, is the self-generated fire of Hell. Whether or not it is the hellfire to which Jesus refers, it is definitely a suffering the soul in Hell experiences.

To vary the analogy, we might compare the soul's attraction to God to a burning thirst. "I must find God, or I will perish!" the soul cries out. Yet he cannot find God, and he cannot perish. Like a man dying of thirst in the desert and running in desperate circles, seeking the spring that he knows to be there but cannot find, so does the soul in Hell search vainly for God.

Souls in Hell have chosen to be there

Added to the anguish of Hell is an excruciating remorse. The person in Hell knows that he is there through his own free choice. God doesn't want anyone in Hell. God made every soul to be with Him in Heaven. When we speak of Hell as a punishment, we must be sure that we understand the way in which we use the word *punishment*. Hell is a punishment, right enough, but it is a self-chosen punishment, like the hangover that a drunkard knowingly chooses for himself.

When we talk of God, we have to talk of Him in human terms; otherwise we could not talk about Him at all. But we have to remember that our human way of talking about God is often inaccurate. For example, we speak of the "anger" of God toward the sinner. Even the inspired writers of the Bible often speak of God's anger.[8] Yet it is obvious that God is incapable of anger as we know it. Anger denotes a change in a person, a change from one state of mind to another. Change means that something has been added or something has been taken away. But God is infinitely perfect; nothing can be added to

---

[8] Cf. Exod. 4:14; Num. 11:1.

Him, and nothing can be taken from Him. He is eternally unchangeable.

When we speak of God's being angry with the sinner, we simply are using a form of verbal shorthand. We are describing a change that has taken place, not in God, but in the person who has sinned. God's love has not ceased to go out to the sinner; the sinner, rather, has placed himself outside the range of God's love. The sun has not stopped shining just because a man has pulled down his window shade and has shut the sunlight out of his room. However, by saying that God is angry, we save words and emphasize the sinner's plight. It is a form of speech that the Holy Spirit Himself has sanctioned.

Similarly, when we speak of God's casting a soul into Hell, we must realize that again we are using literary shorthand. God does not hold some poor, weak, "really didn't mean it" soul over the pit of Hell and say as He drops him in, "All right, chum, you've had it. Now how do you like this?"

Hell, with all its consequences, results from eternal separation from God. This is a separation that only a man himself can effect, by deliberately refusing God his love. Knowing the full consequences of his deed, the sinner chooses to have his cake here rather than to eat it in Heaven. Hell is self-chosen, self-inflicted.

This knowledge that he has only himself to blame for his presence in Hell is "the worm that dieth not."[9] It is the savage, penetrating, biting worm of remorse. The soul in Hell writhes in the bitter knowledge: "I picked this for myself. I was

---

[9] Cf. Mark 9:43, 45.

so smart. I could chisel a bit on God, I figured, and get away with it. I would repent of my sins in my own good time, after I'd had my fun. And anyway, Hell would be worth the fun I was having. That's what I thought, imbecile that I was. Look at me now!"

Hell is a state of unrelieved loneliness, of total hatred, of an eternally frustrated search for God, of torturing remorse. When we have said all this, we have said very little. Words cannot really describe Hell any more than words can describe Heaven. The only one who could describe Hell is the person who is there, and no one has come back to make the attempt. Yet, to the extent that our limited human mind can comprehend it, we need to have a deep-rooted horror of Hell. In a time of severe temptation, a healthy fear of Hell may be the influence that tips the scales, saves us from surrender, and checks our flight from God.

Meditating on Hell, we surely shall heed the plea of our Blessed Mother at Fatima. It was there that she urged us to pray, "O Jesus, forgive us our sins, save us from the fires of Hell; bring all souls to Heaven, especially those who have the greatest need of Thy mercy!" In union with Mary, we shall pray for each other — for deliverance from any waywardness that might separate us from the infinitely loving God.

Chapter Nine

❧

Gain the benefits of Confession

If a priest had a dollar for every time one of his penitents has said, after Confession, "I feel so much better, Father; it's so good to get that weight off my shoulders" (or words to that effect), he would have the price of a new car in a very few years. The load that has been shed may not have been a matter of sin. It may have been a gnawing worry or a painful doubt or scruple. It may have been a personal problem difficult to discuss outside the anonymous secrecy of the confessional. Perhaps you yourself have never put your gratitude into words, but you are not typical if you never have said, even in your heart, "Thank God for Confession!"

In this practical aspect of Confession — the mental peace it confers — we have the simplest answer to our non-Catholic friends when they question us on the matter of Confession. To non-Catholics, even those well-disposed, the sacrament of Penance frequently present a serious stumbling block. You may have heard a non-Catholic say, "There are many things I like about the Catholic Church, but I just can't accept the idea of Confession"; or, "I don't see why I should tell my sins to any other human being. If I do wrong, it's enough to tell God

I'm sorry in the privacy of my own heart"; or, "There's a guy in my office who goes to Confession every month, but he still gets drunk every Saturday night. I just can't understand that."

When we hear such remarks, we should not pass them off with a shrug of the shoulders. Here is an opportunity to use the grace of Confirmation, a chance to be an instrument in the hands of our Lord for the spreading of His truth. If such an opportunity comes to you, you might begin with a scriptural line of reasoning. "Look, Charlie," you might say, "you must admit that if Jesus wants us to tell our sins in order to have them forgiven, we've got to do it His way. We can't pick and choose and say, 'I'd rather do it my way.' "

Then you could go on to explain the significance of Christ's words to His disciples on Easter Sunday night: "Whose sins you shall forgive, they are forgiven them; and whose sins you shall retain, they are retained."[10] You could point out that the second clause here ("whose sins you shall retain") would be superfluous if Jesus did not intend us to tell our sins. How could the Apostles (and the priests who succeed them) know what sins to forgive and what sins to retain (not forgive), if they did not know what the sins were?

Jesus did not use words carelessly. Every word He spoke is pregnant with meaning. There is just no reasonable way to explain His words away, except to conclude that our sins are to be forgiven after a humble confession of them. There is no sin that, by its nature, is unforgivable, if the penitent's sorrow and purpose of amendment are genuine. It is the quality of his

[10] John 20:23.

sorrow and the firmness of his purpose that the priest is able to judge from the penitent's self-revelation.

Then, you could turn to the historical proof of Confession. You could say, "Charlie, read up on ancient Christian history. Dig into the Fathers of the early Church. You'll find that Confession is as old as Christianity. This is the way sins were forgiven from the very beginning. Surely the people who came along right after Christ, two thousand years ago, ought to be the best judges of what Jesus really meant. Confessions always preceded the forgiveness of sins in the Christian world. Martin Luther didn't like Confession, and he got rid of it very quickly when he started the first Protestant church in 1517. We think the Apostles and the early Christians were better judges of Christ's intentions than someone who came along fifteen hundred years later. If the Bible means anything and if history means anything, the sacrament of Penance is Jesus' own doing. We've just got to accept it if we accept Him."

∽

Tell others of the benefits you receive from Confession

If your friend Charlie (or whoever) is a reasonable man, all this would be a sound line of reasoning. However, one of the most powerful recommendations for anything is the recommendation of a satisfied user. Charlie might be more impressed if you simply said, "Look, Charlie, I've been going to Confession for umpteen years. I know the peace of mind it can give me. I know what it means to get a load off my chest. I know what it means to be certain that my sins are forgiven and that I can make a wholly new start in life. If I've got a pain in my belly, I'm mighty glad I can go to a doctor and have an expert tell me whether it's appendicitis or just a bit of gas. In the same way, if I've got a spiritual problem, I'm thankful that I can go with it to an expert for guidance and direction. What makes it especially easy is that this expert isn't going to ask for my name and social security number. He'll just listen to the facts, point out where I'm wrong, and tell me what steps to take. No matter how personal my problem may be, I feel easy about discussing it. I know that I'm talking to a man who is bound by an obligation of secrecy that has no equal in the world. All the tractors in Kansas couldn't pull out of him what I tell him in Confession. Even to save his own life, he can't reveal what I tell.

"I'll tell you another thing, Charlie. I know how easy it is for me to kid myself and to find excuses for myself when I pull a boner. If I could have my sins forgiven just by saying silently, 'God, I'm sorry,' I'm afraid I might not improve much. I could fool myself into thinking I was sorry and still keep going my merry, sinful way. But when I have to get down on my knees and put my wrongdoing into words, it means I've got to face the facts. It's pretty hard then to kid myself or to dodge behind excuses.

"Sure, some people seem to go to Confession without getting much good from it, like that fellow you mentioned who gets drunk every Saturday night. Maybe he's just ignorant about his religion. Maybe he thinks that Confession is a spiritual laundry, where you get rid of one load of dirt so that you can take on another. If he thinks that, of course he's one hundred percent wrong. A person can't even make a good Confession unless he's firmly determined not to commit grave sins again. Without that intention, his sins couldn't possibly be forgiven. He'd have to be a hypocrite to say, 'O my God, I am sorry for my sins,' and still have it in mind to do the same thing again.

"On the other hand, maybe the fellow you mention is just weak. Maybe he wants to do better, and Confession is the one thing that is keeping him from going to pieces entirely. We have to think of that, you know. It's not only a question of how much better a person ought to be with Confession, but also of how much worse he might be without Confession. Maybe in God's eyes that fellow is putting up a real fight. God is the only one who can tell.

"Forgive me for being blunt, Charlie. But when you say that you don't like the idea of Confession, you just don't know what you're talking about. The only one who has the right to talk about Confession is someone who has given it a try. I can tell you that, except maybe for Mass and Holy Communion, Confession is the last thing in the Catholic Church I would want to do without. I'd say to Jesus, 'Take other things away if you must, Lord, but don't take Confession!' When I remember to thank God for all that He has done for me, believe me, the sacrament of Penance is one of the things I always include."

You will agree, I think, that an explanation of this kind may be more meaningful to an inquiring friend than an answer taken from a theology book. Of course, to give the answer and to make it ring true, it must really flow from a person's own experience. He must be someone who understands, highly prizes, and frequently uses the sacrament of Penance. There are too many who do not, and they represent a variety of types.

⚘

Don't let fear or laziness keep you from Confession

One type, fortunately rare, is the person who suffers from confessional-phobia. The moment he enters a confessional, he panics. He feels ill or feels as if he is going to suffocate in the confessional's narrow confines. The problem here is psychological rather than spiritual. A person with this particular difficulty should consult a psychiatrist for assistance. Or at least he should discuss the problem with a priest in the relaxed comfort of the rectory office.

A second class of persons who avoid Confession are the confirmed sinners who have no intention of abandoning their sins. Confession would mean reform, and they have no intention of reforming. Their consciences are too atrophied to realize their deadly state or to pray for a change of heart. Their only hope is that the prayers of family and friends may win for them the grace of repentance before it is too late.

A third type of Catholic who abstains from Confession is one who at some time in the past was the victim of false shame or sudden fear in the confessional, and as a consequence failed to confess a mortal sin. Perhaps several bad confessions have been added to the original one. He now feels so hopelessly entangled that he gives up going to Confession altogether. Such a person should discover the wonderful feeling of relief that will be his if he will just muster up his courage and say in

Confession, "Father, please help me. I made a bad confession once, and I want to straighten things out." The priest has nothing but compassion for such an unhappy penitent and will do all in his power to make easy the act of spiritual renewal.

A fourth type is the person who has become the victim of a sinful habit, and has given up Confession in discouragement. Because he keeps breaking his good resolutions, he thinks he cannot make a good confession. Yet this is the very person who needs Confession most of all. In frequent Confession lies his only hope of victory. As long as he keeps doggedly trying, God is pleased with his efforts, no matter how many times he may seem to fail. Eventually victory will crown his efforts, and, in the meantime, his confessions are good ones.

Then there is the Catholic who is lax or lazy, or both. He just doesn't have enough love for God to make use of the gifts that Jesus died to obtain for us. There are too many other things he wants to do on Saturday or on any other day when confessions are being heard. He may go to Confession for Easter and perhaps for Christmas, but the promises made in the confessional are forgotten by the following week. It is to this type of Catholic that Jesus speaks through St. John: "I know thy works; thou art neither cold nor hot. I would that thou wert cold or hot. But because thou art lukewarm, and neither cold nor hot, I am about to vomit thee out of my mouth."[11]

Finally, there is the poorly instructed Catholic who thinks that Confession is just for the forgiveness of mortal sins.

[11] Apoc. 3:15-16 (RSV = Rev. 3:15-16).

"There's no need for me to go to Confession," he may say. "I haven't committed any big sin." He has not learned, or has forgotten, that the purpose of the sacrament of Penance is to make saints as well as to save sinners. To one who is already free from grave sin, this sacrament gives an increase in sanctifying grace and deepens the spiritual life of the soul. It also gives its own special grace — that "shot in the arm" which inoculates us against temptation. The guarantee against falling into serious sin is to receive this sacrament often. A person intent on spiritual growth will make Confession, if possible, a weekly practice.

If none of these six types applies to you, then indeed you are in a good position to explain Confession to others. From your own frequent confessions you can testify that here indeed is a precious gift from God.

Chapter Ten

❦

Learn to improve your confessions

✣

Once while visiting Spain, I heard of a workman who found an American hundred-dollar bill. It didn't look like much to him. Spanish banknotes are huge affairs, twice the size of American currency. The workman tucked the hundred-dollar bill in his pocket as a souvenir. Several days later, when passing a bank, he stopped in to ask whether his find had any value. He yelped for joy when he was told that it was worth six thousand *pesetas*, the equivalent of about three months' pay for him.

It is not unusual to hear of people who discover that they have unknowingly harbored a treasure. It may be a valuable painting hanging unnoticed on the wall. It may be a priceless antique gathering dust in the attic. It may be forgotten stock certificates that have become worth a fortune. We all get a bit of that "wish it were I" feeling when we read of such incidents.

Unfortunately, many of us right now are undervaluing a treasure that is ours. The treasure is the sacrament of Penance. No doubt we receive this sacrament frequently. We know that Confession is not intended only for the forgiveness of mortal sin. Even though we may already be free from mortal sin, we know that the sacrament of Penance will give us an increase in sanctifying grace. We are mindful, too, that this sacrament gives its own special grace, which is a strengthening against temptation. We go to Confession often because we know that this is the surest way for us to keep from serious sin.

⚬

Don't take Confession for granted

However, at one time or another we may have said to ourselves, "I don't seem to get much out of Confession. I go often because I know I should, but I can't see that it's making me much better. I seem to be telling the same old sins week after week and month after month."

If we ever have spoken this way, or felt this way, it may quite possibly be that we have been taking Confession too much for granted. Through the years, we have let Confession become a routine matter. Our attitude toward it has become very casual. Perhaps it is not so much that the value of the treasure is unrecognized, as that the value has been forgotten.

As a consequence, we come into church on Saturday, hoping that there will not be many others ahead of us at the confessional. We want to get this over with quickly and get on with our more important business. In thirty seconds we are ready for Confession. There is no need to examine our conscience: it will be the same story we have been telling for the past five or ten years. So we tell it again, then rattle off our act of contrition with but half a thought for the meaning of the words we are saying. After Confession we may remain in church long enough to dispose quickly of our penance; or we may decide to let the penance go until tomorrow at Mass. If we have been lucky enough to find no one ahead of us, the whole process, from car back to car, has taken no more than five minutes. Do we recognize a bit of ourselves in this picture?

Penance is a sacrament that Jesus gave to us at the cost of His life. It is a sacrament that a sin-laden world unknowingly longed for through countless thousands of years. It is a sacrament of such inconceivable power that we could not believe it possible — except that God has done it. It is a sacrament that forces God to stand at attention, prepared to dispense to us His mercy and His grace. It is God's own antimissile missile — the weapon God uses against Himself to divert His infinite justice. It is a sacrament in which we approach so close to the divine throne that there is only the screen of our human blindness between God and us.

Penance is all of this. And how do we esteem it? We give to it, all too often, about the same amount of time and attention that we would give to the task of dropping a suit off at the dry cleaner. Quickly in and quickly out. "There, that's done!"

If we seem to find little change in ourselves in spite of our frequent confessions, perhaps we should scrutinize ourselves on two points that are vital to a fruitful confession. One of these points has to do with our sorrow for sin. The other concerns our examination of conscience.

⚜

Develop sorrow for your sins

Every Catholic is familiar with the fact that we cannot make a good confession if we conceal from the priest a mortal sin that should be told. Every Catholic is equally familiar with the fact that we cannot make a good confession unless we have true sorrow for our sins. A person might tell all his mortal sins ever so well. Yet, if there was a single one of those sins he did not intend to give up, his confession would be worse than useless. We know this well.

However, not every Catholic seems to be aware that the amount of grace we receive in Confession depends on the degree of our sorrow. The more grief of heart I have at the thought of my sins, the more grace I will receive in the sacrament of Penance. If I make a hurried preparation for Confession, with little or no effort to rouse myself to a lively sorrow for present and past offenses against God, I am cheating myself out of an incalculable amount of grace. The few minutes that I save are far, far too expensive.

If we feel, then, that we are getting too little out of our confessions, let us begin to spend five or ten minutes in adequate preparation. We might look at the crucifix above the altar and try to imagine what it would be like to have nails driven through our own hands and feet. We might try, each of us, to make real to ourselves the load of *our own* sins that Jesus bears on His shoulders on the Cross. We might try to force ourselves to look back to some of those pages in our life that we have been trying to forget and which still can bring a blush to our cheek. This does not necessarily mean sins against chastity. How about my sins against charity? How about the time (or times) I so brutally hurt the feelings of another? The time another badly needed help, and I was too selfish to give it? The time I caused trouble and heartache to others by my obstinacy or my pride? The times I gave way to vicious outbursts of temper? The times I helped the Devil in his work by giving bad example? The times I was dishonest or intemperate or rebellious against God's Providence?

There is something in the past that I am ashamed of. Let me drag it out now where I can see it, and let me feel the shame. I do not recall it to torture myself. I recall it only to remind myself of my past ingratitude to God and of my betrayals of Him. What I am seeking is to rouse myself to a new peak of sorrow. Then, when I have told this week's little sins, there will be real meaning in my words when I say, "I am also sorry for all the sins of my past life." Grace will flow in abundance into my soul.

❧

Examine your conscience thoroughly

A hurried preparation for Confession results not only in skimpy sorrow; it results also in a skimpy examination of conscience. What we told the priest last time should not be the same story we tell him again today. Perhaps we are forgetting that, if it is the same old sins we keep telling over and over, we might as well not tell them at all.

Even venial sins cannot be forgiven without true sorrow for them and a purpose of amendment. If we are committing the same sins week after week with no noticeable improvement, the genuineness of our sorrow is very questionable. It would be better not to mention them at all than to say untruthfully that we are sorry for them. Here again it is evident that our sorrow needs working on.

Undoubtedly, the examination of conscience needs working on as well. In a few seconds we cannot possibly make a thorough and honest appraisal the past several days. This is why our daily faults and failures succeed in escaping attention. This is why we can say, and think it true, "I just can't seem to remember any sins since last time."

Oh no? How about the judgments we have passed on others in our own mind? How about the suspicious thoughts we have entertained? How about those little outbursts of impatience and those complaints that really were a form of opposition to God's will? How about the sharp and thoughtless words we have spoken, the unasked-for criticisms and the unnecessary rebukes? How about wasting our employer's time, or, what is worse, wasting God's time when there are things to be done? How about unnecessary extravagance with family funds? How about the encouragement we have given to gossip by listening?

These questions are proposed merely as suggestions. The point of them is that there are probably more sins in our days than we have realized. We have not recognized those sins because we have not taken the time to go over our days with a fine-tooth comb. It is no wonder, then, that a five-minute "quickie" confession seems to leave us unimproved. It is little wonder if we say, "My confessions don't seem to help me. I don't seem to get any better."

Penance is a sacrament of limitless possibilities for spiritual growth. And it *is* a sacrament, a divine action, sacred and awesome. To it we must bring a great sense of reverence. To it we must give the time and thought that it merits. With growth in sorrow and with a better realization of the fact that we do sin, there also will come a deeper sense of gratitude to God for His sacrament of Reconciliation. We shall no longer be in such a hurry to leave church. Our penance will seem much too small. Our prayers of thanksgiving to Jesus will seem much too inadequate for the graces that have come to us in His sacrament of love-restored and infidelity-forgotten.

Chapter Eleven

Receive Communion

❧

At the Last Supper, the mind of Jesus might well have been completely absorbed by the prospect of the ordeal that lay ahead of Him. Certainly if you or I knew that we were just hours away from a night of savage torture and a death by crucifixion, we would be able to think of nothing else. Yet Jesus thought only of you and me. In His visible body He had to leave the world, but He had a desperate desire to keep close to us.

In His divine mind, He canvassed the possible ways in which He could, as long as men shall live, reach them with His love. His solution was so sensational that only God could have conceived it, so miraculous that only God could do it. He would give us Himself under the appearance of bread and wine. We would not merely adore Him at a distance, as at the Elevation of the Mass or at Benediction of the Blessed Sacrament. Jesus wanted to be closer to us than that. He wanted to get right inside of us, to make us flesh of His Flesh and blood of His Blood. He wanted to enfold us in an embrace more complete and more intimate than man had ever known before. And so He decreed that He should give Himself to us in the act of mutual oneness that we call Holy Communion.

There He now stands at Mass, with His arms outstretched to us. In the Mass He has just renewed the offering of Himself to God the Father, the offering He made for us upon the Cross. He has just gone to the Father to collect for us the graces that, ever since Calvary, have been kept for us. Now He faces us and says, "Come, you whom I love so much. Come and accept the graces I have won for you. Let me enter, not merely your bloodstream, but, by a divine osmosis, let me enter into the very depths of your soul. I shall give you new life, new strength. I shall fortify the bond between you and me. Come, *please* come! Open your heart to me!"

❖

Receive Holy Communion
for the right reasons

Aside from the required (and very minimal) hour-long fast before receiving, all that is required for a worthy Holy Communion is that I have been absolved from mortal sin, if any, in the sacrament of Penance and that I have a right motive in receiving Holy Communion. We have seen the unselfish motive for receiving Holy Communion: because Jesus wants us to. There are, of course, many other motives that are highly worthy, even if more self-interested.

There is, for example, our desire to make certain of our eternal happiness. Jesus has promised, "He who eats my Flesh and drinks my Blood has life everlasting, and I will raise him up at the last day."[12] Frequent Holy Communion is the surest

---

[12] John 6:55 (RSV = John 6:54).

of all sure paths to Heaven. There is also the very wholesome desire to keep out of Hell. Jesus has warned, "Unless you eat the Flesh of the Son of Man, and drink His Blood, you shall not have life in you."[13]

Our attainment of Heaven and our avoidance of Hell are the consequences of the work that Jesus does in our soul when we receive Him in Holy Communion. He helps us to grow in love for God. Our growth in love may not manifest itself emotionally, but it will show in our firmer determination to do God's will. Our Lord also intensifies in us that sharing in God's own life which we call sanctifying grace. Making Himself our spiritual food, He does for our soul what ordinary food does for our body. He gives us the vigorous health we need to resist contagion: to conquer temptation and to reject sin. He helps us to grow in love for our neighbor and to perform works of charity with greater ease.

All of these are excellent reasons for receiving Holy Communion frequently. But the best and most unanswerable is still "because Jesus wants me to."

⚛

The effects of Communion
may not be evident

Someone may object, "I receive Holy Communion often, and I can't see that it makes a bit of difference in my life. I can't see that I'm any better than I was a year ago." One answer to that objection is "Yes, but how much worse might you

---

[13] John 6:54 (RSV = John 6:53).

be if you were not receiving Holy Communion often?" A still better answer is that we are poor judges of our own spiritual state. The very one who thinks he is advancing the fastest may be, in God's eyes, the most laggard. Your humility in thinking you are not as good as you ought to be may itself be an indication that your frequent union with Jesus is having its effect.

If we are among the many who receive Communion at every Mass we attend, we will do well to leave it to Jesus to measure what is happening in our soul — and in the soul of our neighbor. It is enough to know that we are giving Him the pleasure of our company. Quite simply, it is enough that when He says, "Come to me!" we come.

Chapter Twelve

⚘

Fulfill your role
in the Mass

%

Do you enjoy going to Mass? It is not essential that you be able to answer yes to that question. You may be a very good Catholic and still feel that attendance at Mass is something of a penance. After all, the primary purpose of the Mass is not to give pleasure to us, but to give glory to God. If you assist at Mass faithfully only from a sense of duty, you are performing an act that is pleasing to God, even though you might feel relieved when it is finished.

However, if we really understand the nature of the Mass and our part in it, normally we should feel a great sense of satisfaction from our presence there. We should find the Mass anything but boring. Unfortunately, to many Catholics the Mass is a routine Sunday chore. They attend Mass in a spirit of obedience and do gain grace from the dutiful discharge of their obligation. Yet the Mass does not make the impact on their lives that it should.

An understanding of the Mass begins with an understanding of our relationship with God. God made us. We are His property, from head to toe and to the innermost recesses of our souls. Every breath we draw belongs to God. He is everything.

We are nothing except what He has made us to be. We have nothing except what He has given us. If God could forget us (which He cannot), in the instant of His forgetting, we would cease to be.

We must acknowledge the completeness of our dependence on Him who made us and who supports us in our existence. The very nature of our relationship of creature to Creator demands this of us. If you are a parent, you can get a faint understanding of this duty from your own expectations of your children. When young, children are thoughtless and inclined to take things for granted. As they grow older, however, you hope they will have some understanding of all you have tried to do for them. You are pleased when they show some signs of gratitude for the sacrifices you have made for them. You will probably never put this expectation into words. Yet, if your children seemed to assume they were self-made and owed you nothing, you would be a most unhappy parent.

God has an even greater right to an acknowledgment from us of His supreme position in our lives. He has an even greater right to receive from us a confession of His infinite greatness and goodness and of our dependence on Him. He has an even greater right to an expression from us of our gratitude for all He has done for us. He has an even greater right to some show of love from us in return for the love He has poured without measure on us.

We partially fulfill this obligation whenever we pray. However, from time without memory, men have felt that something more than words is needed to do justice to this duty. There is an instinct in us that urges, "Let us not just say it. Let us do something to show that we mean it!" So, from the days of Cain and Abel, man has "acted out" his role of creature. He has acted it out through the giving of gifts to God. Choosing the best from all that God has bestowed, has offered back to God the best fruits of his flocks, of his fields, and of his handiwork. This acting out of man's duty to God has been signalized by a special name. The name is *sacrifice*, which means "something made sacred" — made sacred because it has been set apart and given to God.

An action we do is always more expressive and emphatic than words we say. God showed His pleasure in this form of prayer-in-action by commanding, in the Old Testament, certain prescribed forms of sacrifice. Sheep and lambs were to be offered to Him, and goats and bullocks, and bread and wine. These were poor tokens to be presenting to God. He already has everything, and He Himself created these gifts in the first place. But they were the best that man could give, and God was pleased.

Then Jesus came into the world. Being a man, He could speak for men. In His humanity, *all* humanity was in a sense contained. No one was better equipped to act out the drama of man's duty to God. It is a drama in which the words, spoken or unspoken, always are the same: "My God, You are my all. I bow down before You. I surrender myself wholly to You. I give You my will and my love. All that I have has come from You, and I thank You for it. I grieve that I have misused Your gifts so often, and I beg to atone for my many infidelities."

As *the* man, the summation in one person of the whole human race, Jesus could act this out for all of us for all time. He did act it out — on the Cross. There His gift was not of animals or of grain or of fruit. It was the gift of Himself. And it was not merely the gift of His physical self that He offered. That would have been more than enough. Since Jesus is God, one single drop of His Blood is infinite in its value. One sigh of His Sacred Heart would have meant more to God than ten thousand mountains of sheep and goats. However, Jesus offered the *whole* of Himself in one tremendous act of obedient love: "Not my will, but Thine be done."[14]

The Mass lets you offer Christ's Sacrifice

In His role of the universal man, Jesus could offer Himself for each of us, but only if we were willing to have Him represent us. He had to provide some way in which we could add our *amen* to what He was doing. He had to give us an opportunity to write our name on the gift He was offering to God. And so, the night before He died, at the Last Supper, He instituted the Sacrifice of the Mass.

Like a million wires stretching out from a central switchboard, the Mass reaches down from Calvary, through the centuries, to each soul. In the Mass, each of us can give his free consent and approval to the gift Jesus offered on the Cross in our name. We can add our act of adoration and of love to His. Each of us has the opportunity to speak his own *amen*.

This has been, admittedly, much too brief a description of what happens at Mass. It is intended only as a reminder, not as

[14] Luke 22:42.

an adequate explanation. Its purpose is to set the scene for our assistance at Mass.

As we enter the church for Mass, on Sundays or weekdays, it would be a great mistake for us to feel that we are coming simply to watch the priest perform a holy action. It would be a great mistake for us to consider ourselves as patient or even pious onlookers. No, we are coming to perform a holy action *ourselves*. It is an action of crucial importance, an action that no one else, not even Jesus, can do for us. The Mass is our direct and open line to Calvary, and through Calvary to Heaven. We have come to say, "Present and accounted for" to Jesus on the Cross. We have come to sign our name on the Gift. We have come to speak our vehement *amen!*

There is one point in the Mass where our role is beautifully expressed. This point occurs at the very end of the Consecration of the Mass — just before the Our Father.

With the Sacred Host in his hand, the priest says, "Through Him [that is, Jesus], with Him, and in Him, in the unity of the Holy Spirit, all glory and honor is Yours, Almighty Father, forever and ever." The priest raises the chalice and Sacred Host above the altar in what is called the "Little Elevation," and the entire congregation, gazing upon the upraised chalice and Host, thunders out, "Amen." It is called the "Great Amen" of the Mass. It is the congregation's opportunity to express vocally their wholehearted agreement and personal participation in all that has been done. In this *amen* is contained the whole mood and spirit in which we should assist at Mass.

We come into church, then, aware that God our Creator, God our Father, is waiting to receive our act of homage. The

Mass begins, and we take our stand beside Jesus as He prepares, through His human priest, to re-enact the great Sacrifice, the Gift, of Himself on Calvary. The Mass is the group gift of Christ's whole family — most meaningful when we pray or sing it together; however, this is not essential. What is essential to us is that throughout the Mass we have a "me too!" attitude. Whether we pray together or individually, all through the Mass we are conscious of God the Father, who waits for us, and of God the Son, who acts for us. Our enduring intention is, "Yes, Jesus. Yes, yes, yes! You can speak for me. I give myself, with You, to God completely. Take my love, make it a part of Yours. Let myself be a little bit of the Gift You offer."

This is what the Mass should mean for us. If we come into church with this awareness of our importance to Jesus in what is about to take place, the Mass can never be tedious or boring. If there was ever a time for us to be fully alive, alert, and with a sense of important achievement, it is at Mass. If, in the past, our mental state at Mass has been one of penitential obedience, it may be because we have forgotten how much our willing presence there can mean, to Jesus and to the Father. It may well be that, once we have fully grasped the grandeur and the vital importance of our role, once-a-week Mass will no longer satisfy us.

Chapter Thirteen

⁂

Learn to pray well

❧

While visiting New Mexico some years ago, I met a man who was very despondent. He spent his spare time prospecting for silver and had staked a claim in an area where he had found silver-bearing rock. On weekends and holidays he had blasted and picked a hole in the mountainside until he had accumulated enough rock for the assay office. He had just received a report from the assay office. It said that his sample was too low in silver content to justify commercial exploitation. His many days of hard labor had been wasted.

If we could send a specimen of our prayers to a heavenly assay office, we might face a similar disappointment. The report might say that in our piled-up words there was not enough real prayer to justify all the time and labor we had expended.

There are two things that determine the quality of our prayer: the *attention* and the *intention* with which we pray.

❧

Pray attentively
We are familiar enough with the need for attention. This was pretty well drilled into us in our childhood catechism

lessons. We know there is no magic in mere words. Jesus Himself warned us against this fallacy. "In praying," He said, "do not multiply words, as the Gentiles do; for they think that by saying a great deal, they will be heard. So do not be like them; for your Father knows what you need before you ask Him."[15]

Our Lord is not condemning prayers of petition. Many times over, He made it plain that God is pleased to have us ask Him for help. Even though He knows our needs, God rejoices to have us acknowledge our dependence on Him. Every time we turn to God for a grace or favor, we are saluting Him as the source of all good and as the loving Father that He is.

What our Lord condemns is purely mechanical prayer: the repetition of words as though there were a value in the words themselves regardless of our state of mind. We find this view of prayer carried to a logical extreme among the Lamaists of Asia. They cover a wheel with prayers, then spin the wheel. They consider that the prayers have been said once with each turn of the wheel. Our very definition of prayer as "a raising of the mind and heart to God" exposes the absurdity of such a practice. Words, written or spoken, are only symbols. It is the sentiments of mind and heart that give them whatever meaning and value they may have.

Knowing this, we do not undertake to pray unless we are ready to give attention to what we are doing. Even then, we realize that it is attention to God, rather than attention to the words, that is the important thing. Words are but the track or road over which my spirit travels to God. Words are simply the

[15] Matt. 6:7-8.

means by which I include my body in my act of worship, so that it is the *whole* person — mind and body — who prays.

For example, I may pray the litany of the Sacred Heart of Jesus as an act of thanksgiving to our Lord for His innumerable goodnesses to me. Through the entire litany, my grateful heart may be thinking of nothing but His loving generosity. My mind may hardly advert to the actual meaning of the words I am saying, yet I am praying well. On the other hand, I might foolishly give such slavish attention to the literal meaning of the individual words as to have little attention left for Jesus Himself.

We know that the attention required in prayer is not nullified by the involuntary distractions that plague us all. The human mind is as unstable as a little child: restless, squirming, running from one thing to another, incapable of sustained effort. We may approach prayer with a firm determination to pray well and to keep our mind on what we are doing. Three minutes later we find that our mind has wandered off on some silly expedition of its own. If we are ill, tired, worried, or excited, these distractions are likely to be thrice aggravated.

Pray with a right intention

However, this does not discourage us. We know that our prayer is still acceptable to God, even if we spend the whole time doing nothing else but brushing away distractions. Indeed, this prayer may be *especially* pleasing to God, by the very fact that we are praying under such difficulties. As long as we have undertaken to pray with a right intention, and with an honest effort to give God the best attention we can, our prayer is most acceptable to Him.

Right intention is a key phrase here. In general, we pray because God wants us to pray. It is a duty we creatures owe to our Creator. If for no other reason, we pray from a sense of obedience and to discharge a grave obligation to God. From this basic reason for prayer, we can see how foolish it would be for anyone to excuse himself from prayer on the score that he does not feel like praying. Prayer is not a matter of mood, any more than it is a matter of convenience. We never can justify lack of prayer by pleading that we have no time for it. We must — absolutely *must* — find the time for prayer.

Even less can we justify lack of prayer by the absence of a feeling for prayer, or by the fact that we do not seem to "get anything out of prayer." We do not pray in order to get something out of it. We pray because God wants us to. Emotionally we may feel as cold as an iceberg. We may rise from prayer without any sense whatever of uplift or inspiration. It doesn't matter. Prayer is something we do primarily for God. What we may get out of it is very secondary. Our prayer may be dry and unrewarding to ourselves; it still has been pleasing to God.

Turning from this general intention of discharging our duty to God, there are some more specific intentions that are called for in prayer:

• *Petition:* In spite of our catechism lessons of long ago, many of us persist in viewing prayer as principally a matter of asking God for what we want. We have already observed that this is one purpose of prayer, and a good purpose, too. However, in rank of importance, it holds last place. A person who confined his prayers exclusively to prayers of petition would stand little chance of having his petitions heard. Unless he has prefaced his petitions with the more substantial prayer of adoration, thanksgiving, and repentance, his appeals scarcely qualify as prayer. If God never sees us except with our hand out, we have little claim on the bounty of God. Being who He is, He may have pity on our ignorance or patience with our selfishness, but our prayers will be low-grade ore indeed.

◆ *Adoration:* We have said that prayer is a duty we owe to God. The first element in that duty is that we give to the infinitely great, good, and holy God the adoration that is His due. We stand before Him with awe and reverence, creatures before their Creator, children in the presence of their Father. In love and in humility, our heart bows to Him. We tell Him of our love for Him, we acknowledge our dependence on Him, we pledge Him our to-the-death loyalty and obedience. Understanding that He is all-wise and knows what is best for us, all-loving and wants only what is best for us, we assure Him that we shall try to make His will our own.

All these sentiments are merged in our act of adoration. In terms of set prayers, acts of faith, hope, and love such as the following are par excellence prayers of adoration:

❧

Act of Faith

O my God, I firmly believe that Thou art
one God in three divine Persons —
Father, Son, and Holy Spirit.
I believe that Thy divine Son became man,
died for our sins, and that He will come
to judge the living and the dead.
I believe these and all the truths which the holy
Catholic Church teaches, because Thou hast revealed
them, who canst neither deceive nor be deceived.

❧

Act of Hope

O my God, relying on Thy almighty power
and infinite mercy and promises,
I hope to obtain pardon of my sins,
the help of Thy grace, and life everlasting,
through the merits of Jesus Christ,
my Lord and my Redeemer.

❧

Act of Love

O my God, I love Thee above all things,
with my whole heart and soul,
because Thou art all good and worthy of all love.
I love my neighbor as myself for the love of Thee.
I forgive all who have injured me and
ask pardon of all whom I have injured.

Learn to pray well

Other prayers of adoration are our Lord's own prayer, the Our Father, as well as the *Gloria* of the Mass, the Apostles' and Nicene Creeds, and any other prayer that speaks God's praises, such as litanies, psalms, and aspirations. Prayers in honor of our Blessed Mother and the saints also are, indirectly, prayers of adoration to God. In honoring the saints, we honor God, whose masterpieces of grace they are.

• *Thanksgiving:* After adoration, the most urgent objective of prayer is thanksgiving. Our prayers of thanksgiving should be at least as numerous as our prayers of petition. But if we never addressed to God a prayer of petition, we would still have a wealth of gifts to thank Him for. We thank Him for having made us and for having given us this chance for eternal life. We thank Him for having redeemed us and for having forgiven us our sins. We thank Him for the grace of faith He has given us, undeservedly. We thank Him for the saving graces He has given us in moments of temptation, and for having removed, unknown to us, so many temptations from our path. We thank Him for our family and our friends, for health and success, and for the meritorious crosses of our illnesses and failures. Most of all we thank Him, as we do in the *Gloria* of the Mass, for just being the glorious God that He is.

Any prayers we choose to say may be addressed to God as prayers of thanksgiving. Our Fathers, Hail Marys, Rosaries, litanies, novenas, and favorite devotions: all can have the spirit of thanksgiving behind them. However, once in a while, to keep ourselves mindful, we should address to God a simple prayer of thanksgiving in our own words, mentioning some of the specific benefits for which we are particularly thankful.

• *Contrition:* We have adored God in His great and holy goodness. We have recalled and acknowledged our debt of gratitude to Him. Almost automatically our next intention will form itself. In spite of everything, we have abused God's love. Time and again we have slapped away His outstretched hand and have chosen self in preference to Him. We have sinned. Now, conscious of the enormity of our rebellion, we tell Him of our sorrow. An act of contrition rises almost spontaneously to our lips. Included in our sorrow will be a renewed purpose to avoid sin and all that might lead to sin.

Flowing from our sorrow will be acts of reparation: prayers, Masses, and deeds of charity and self-denial offered in atonement for our sins. Inspired by our love for God, to whom souls are so precious, we shall find joy in offering acts of atonement for others also. We shall seek to win the grace of repentance for sinners who are too blind or too hardened to seek repentance for themselves.

※

Pray daily

Praying with attention and with the right intention, we shall discover the power that resides in genuine prayer. And we shall pray, God grant, with conscientious regularity. We shall never begin our day without sanctifying it with prayer, without speaking our "good morning" to God. Time may be short, but it takes only a moment to say, "O my God, I adore You, I love You, I thank You for the new day that You have given me. I beg of You the graces I will need to live this day for You and to live it well." We may expand upon these sentiments as time permits, but God will always have His morning greeting.

And no matter how tired, we shall never close our eyes in sleep without first thanking God for the graces of the day that is past, or without asking His forgiveness for the sins and the failures of the day. At other times, surely, there will be other prayers — frequently reinforced, let us hope, with a simple petition: "Dear Lord, help me to pray well."

Chapter Fourteen

❧

Be courageous and compassionate

⚜

George was a man who was greatly blessed in life. He had good and loving parents and a happy childhood. He had a quick mind and did well in school. He was successful in his work and enjoyed a comfortable income. He married a woman with a happy disposition, who was a topnotch homemaker and saw her husband as the finest man God ever made. His home was in a pleasant, quiet neighborhood. In short, George lived in a fairly tranquil atmosphere with few frustrations or tensions. He led a blameless life and enjoyed a well-deserved reputation as a man of virtue.

Joe was a man of different caliber. His childhood was full of insecurity, with parents who argued incessantly and who were constantly threatening to separate. Whether from emotional strain or from lack of learning power, Joe did consistently poor work in school. He was in the principal's office often and finally graduated only through the charity of his teachers. He held a routine job that just barely provided enough to pay the bills. With no financial margin of safety, Joe worried about the possibility of losing his job and about the possible disaster of a major illness or accident. He lived in a less desirable neighborhood, with the houses close together and the noise considerable. His wife was a poor manager and a nagger besides. Joe frequently drank too much, had an explosive temper, and was much given to profanity — definitely not a candidate for Virtuous Man of the Year.

George and Joe both went to church regularly. George was a frequent communicant, while Joe received the sacraments at less regular intervals. In due time, both men died and appeared before God in judgment. Both got to Heaven, but both experienced some surprises in the process. George's big surprise was to find that he did not stand as high on God's roster as he had expected. "Yes, you were good," was God's verdict, "but why shouldn't you have been? Your life fell along pleasant lines with very few worries or problems. By nature you were a man of moderate passions with comparatively few temptations. Is it any credit to yourself that your life was virtuous? Really you should have been a great saint."

Joe was surprised to find that he had made the grade at all. He was even more surprised to find that he was several degrees above George in glory. "You could have done better" was the judgment he heard, "but you stayed in there, fighting. You didn't give in to self-pity and make your tough breaks an excuse for surrender. Considering your weaknesses and your handicaps, you didn't do too badly with the graces I gave you."

This little parable of George and Joe is intended to illustrate a truth we sometimes forget: that there is much more to sin and virtue than appears on the surface. If all men were born with exactly the same endowments, if all men were nurtured and reared in exactly the same kind of environment, if all men had exactly the same kind of opportunities and faced temptations of exactly the same strength, then we could safely make comparisons and say, "This man is good. That man is bad." Life, however, is not that simple. So only God can know the relative virtue of any individual. Only God can know how hard each one has tried, in view of his own particular personality and his own particular problems, to use the graces God has given.

Persevere in using God's grace

Understanding this, we should take courage. Each of us has his own handicaps. Few of us come to adulthood with a perfectly balanced personality. Few of us escape all scars in the process of growing up. Moreover, our passions may be strong and our judgment warped. Our living conditions may be harassed and our associates disagreeable. Our worries may be numerous and our tensions constant. God knows all this. Of each of us He asks only that we do the best we can with what we have. He asks only that we keep stubbornly trying, no matter how often we may seem to fail or to slip back. It is not so much a complete victory that God looks for from us as a dogged perseverance in our efforts to achieve victory. We might say that it is the trying, rather than the getting, that God judges us by.

It may be that none of this applies to us. It may be that we have enjoyed many advantages in life that make it fairly easy for us to be good. Then depend on it: God expects more than ordinary goodness from us. He knows our assets as well as He knows our handicaps. We dare not let ourselves rest upon that level of virtue which "comes natural" to us.

However, there probably are more of us who need encouragement in our struggle than there are those who need a prick of the spurs. And we do find encouragement in the knowledge that God understands and duly assesses all the influences that enter into our decisions and our deeds.

Be compassionate toward others

Along with increased courage in our own efforts to do God's will, there should be a corresponding growth in our understanding of our neighbor and his problems. This means that we shall be quicker to make allowances for the weaknesses and the mistakes of our fellowman. Words of harsh criticism seldom will be heard upon our lips. We shall remember that, with our advantages, we are probably not doing as much for God as the person who, with his handicaps, seems to do much less. The man or woman I am tempted to condemn may stand far higher in God's eyes than I do.

We do not know all the hidden influences that affect our neighbor's actions. We do not know the kind of home and parents he may have had, the inadequacies of childhood training or the inner wounds he may have suffered. God knows all these things and takes them into account in His judgment. I do not know them; therefore I dare not make myself the judge of my neighbor's virtue.

Certainly I cannot condone, as though they did not matter, the sinful actions my neighbors may commit. But, with compassion strong within me, my attitude toward the errant one will be that of pity rather than contempt. It will be a prayer for him, rather than abuse of him, that my mouth shall speak. Compassion is, indeed, a most essential ingredient in my practice of charity toward my fellows. And I can easily measure the degree of my compassion by the frequency of my unkind criticisms of others.

Compassion was one of our Lord's most striking characteristics during His life on earth. At Jacob's well, there was His gentle treatment of the Samaritan woman who was living with a man not her husband.[16] There was His gentle patience toward the reputedly dishonest publicans. There was His forgiving dismissal of the woman convicted of adultery.[17] There was His compassion toward Mary Magdalen, toward the ambitious brothers James and John, toward the cowardly Peter and the doubting Thomas.[18]

The Pharisees were the only ones toward whom Jesus was severe. These were men who had every advantage of family, training, and high position, yet they condemned and oppressed those who were less fortunate than they. Because He was God and could read hearts, Jesus had the right to judge the Pharisees.

We, however, have no such right. When bitter words rise to our lips, we remember that we are not God. We cannot read hearts. We can only be compassionate — and silent.

[16] Cf. John 4:6-26.
[17] Cf. John 8:3-11.
[18] Cf. Luke 7:36-50; Mark 10:35-45; John 21:15-19, 20:24-28.

The woman next door is a sloppy housekeeper. Yes, but did she have the training I had? Does she have my mental and emotional health?

That man down the street is such a braggart. I get tired of hearing him talk about himself. Yes, but what hidden battle is he fighting? From what deep feelings of inferiority does his bragging flow?

The woman across the alley is such a bore. She can talk only about her aches and pains and troubles. Yes, but what did she miss in her childhood that makes it so necessary now for her to seek attention and sympathy?

The man I work for is so domineering — a slave driver if I ever saw one. Yes, but what twist of fortune left him so inwardly insecure that he must constantly bolster himself up with an overbearing manner?

In the compassionate person, it is considerations such as these that quiet the impulse to criticize and condemn.

Courage and compassion will bring you happiness

Courage and compassion! These are twin virtues that can make the practice of our religion a satisfying and joyful experience. We are courageous and cheerful in our own spiritual efforts because we remember that God does not ask of us more than we are able to give. He knows our capabilities, but He knows our handicaps, too. We do our honest best and are confident that God will be satisfied with that.

Toward our neighbors we are gentle, kind, and understanding. Our compassion makes us ever mindful of their hidden disadvantages, the disabilities and defects that can be known only to God. And in our practice of compassion we discover, perhaps with some surprise, that charitableness is so much more fun than harsh judgment and criticism. In faultfinding and vindictive criticism, there is a venom that corrodes and destroys the heart of the one who sits in judgment on his fellows. In compassion there is a constructiveness, a creativity that brings a sense of achievement to the understanding soul — almost a feeling of exhilaration. Because of our compassion, we are happier persons, and there are few virtues, incidentally, that will bring us so close to the Heart of Christ.

Chapter Fifteen

Attend to others' needs

Time and again in the Gospels, Jesus drives home the truth that we do not love Him unless we love our neighbor. We must be as individual cells in the human body, working together for the good of each other and for the good of the entire body. As members of Christ's Mystical Body, we dare not be unmindful of each other. On the night that His Passion began, Jesus prayed for us: "That they all may be one, even as Thou, Father, in me and I in Thee; that they also may be one in us."[19]

Be concerned for others

We Catholics in America share with our fellow citizens the spirit of individualism. We are Catholics, but we are the product of the culture in which we live; and the American culture is one of competition rather than cooperativeness. "Get ahead, and stay ahead!" "Don't be a spoke in the wheel!" "Live your own life!" "Develop your own personality!" "Dare to be different!" These are some of the catchphrases we have

---

[19] John 17:21.

been listening to through the years. We would be less than human if we have not been influenced to some extent by these repeated exhortations to rugged individualism. And we *have* been influenced, most of us. We have come to focus our attention almost wholly on ourselves and our own family, the latter being but an extension of ourselves.

Neither as Americans nor as Catholics are we hard-hearted by nature. Indeed, if we go to excess, it is more likely to be on the side of sentimentality than on the side of callousness. Let the newspapers mention a child who is doomed to die of cancer, and the child will be deluged with cards and with gifts. Let there be a disaster such as a tornado, fire, or flood, and the sympathy of the nation will go out to the sufferers. Even a condemned murderer can count on a flood of mail going to the governor's office to beg for a reprieve.

No, we are not calloused — merely forgetful. We give baskets to the poor at Thanksgiving and fill stockings at Christmas, but we forget that the poor are poor all year, not just during the holidays. We do not mean to be selfish. We are just too preoccupied with our own interests and activities to think about others, unless their need is called violently to our attention.

I remember a man I met at the wake of his best friend. "I could shoot myself," the man said as he gazed at his friend's corpse. "It was worry that brought on Joe's heart attack; financial worry that killed him. I had a dozen hints, but I never really noticed. I could have helped him and eased his worries and saved his life. But I was too wrapped up in myself to see it."

This gentleman, I am afraid, spoke for many of us. We are too engrossed in our own worries to notice that others have worries, perhaps far greater than ours. We are too busy grappling with our own problems to see how often and how easily we could help to ease the burdens of others. Yet, the more exclusively we let ourselves be enmeshed in our own interests, the farther away we drift from Jesus.

Christ's whole life was one of concern for others — concern that was not limited to matters spiritual. He was never too busy in His mission of teaching, never too deep in His own pain to notice the needs of others. At the pool of Bethsaida He paused to cure the man who was too crippled to lower himself into the healing waters.[20] At Naim He made the widow's heart rejoice when He restored her son to her.[21] He dried the tears of Mary and Martha by raising their brother Lazarus to life.[22] He stopped on the way to Calvary to pity and comfort the women whose children would perish in the approaching destruction of Jerusalem.[23] On the Cross He prayed for His executioners.[24] It was always others and their needs that weighed most heavily on His mind.

∝

Give of your time and attention
If we wish to test our closeness to Jesus and our oneness with Him, we have only to ask ourselves, "How much concern

[20] John 5:2-9.
[21] Luke 7:11-15.
[22] John 11:17-44.
[23] Luke 23:27-28.
[24] Luke 23:34.

do I feel for others? How much of myself do I devote to their needs?" It may be that our material means are very limited. We are already generous in our giving and truthfully can say that we can give no more. However, money is probably the least of the demands that charity makes upon us. Most of us will gladly give money to relieve distress if this will absolve us from the need to think about the distress. Most of us will much more willingly give money to aid a cause if this will free us from giving time to the cause. To most of us, thought (for our own interests and problems) and time (for our own activities and affairs) are much more precious than money.

An example of this was illustrated at an Altar Society meeting. During the coffee hour following the meeting, a member mentioned that her new baby was due in a few days. She said that she was desperate to find someone to take care of her family while she would be in the hospital. Her search for a temporary housekeeper had so far been in vain. If this young mother had said that she could not afford a housekeeper during her confinement, I am confident that the other ladies would gladly have taken up a collection among themselves to assist her. However, although there were older women present who had no small children of their own, no one attempted to take up a collection of hours. Dividing up the time, they easily could have cared for the young mother's little ones for a few days. There were many words of sympathy, but hours were too precious to share.

Once we develop a feeling of concern for others, we begin to see needs that we never observed before. We find that the opportunities for the practice of Christian charity are almost innumerable. For one thing, our prayers will be greatly enriched by the addition of many new intentions. As our newly opened eyes take note of the misfortunes and problems of others, we shall find much to pray for. We shall pray that out-of-work Mr. Brown finds a new job; that Mary Jones will break up with the divorced man she is dating; that Mrs. Smith will return to the practice of her religion; that Mr. White will join Alcoholics Anonymous and conquer the bottle; that the Johnson couple will establish peace in their home and stop threatening divorce; that our pastor and bishop will have divine guidance in their work and the grace to be holy men; that missionaries will be given courage, and their people the gift of faith. Our list will grow, from day to day. And our prayers for ourselves and our loved ones will be twice as acceptable to God because of the charity we have extended to others.

Our charity, of course, will not end with prayer. There also will be things to do. We may notice that the Martin children are not getting to catechism class. Besides praying for the parents, we shall ask the mother's permission to take her children to the weekly instruction class. Old Mrs. French frequently misses Mass on Sunday because it is hard for her to ride the bus. We shall happily offer to pick her up each Sunday and drive her to church. With their five small children, the young Morton couple are completely housebound. We shall offer to babysit for them one or two evenings a month so that they may have an evening out together. We may remember, with some compunction, poor Mr. Carter, who has been bedridden for months. We shall start paying him an occasional visit, with a magazine, a few flowers, or a bit of fruit in hand. There are so many ways in which we can bring grace and happiness into the lives of others, once we begin to notice. And how we shall rejoice the Heart of our Lord!

Our Christ-like concern will extend beyond the level of prayer and the area of the neighborhood. We shall become more conscious of our responsibilities as a member of the parish community. We shall not so easily shrug off the pastor's repeated and sometimes discouraged appeals for help. It may be a call for more ushers or more choir members. It may be a plea for men and women to teach catechism or to do follow-up work as members of the Confraternity of Christian Doctrine. It may be an invitation to join the St. Vincent de Paul Society, the Legion of Mary, the Christian Family Movement, or some other apostolic group. No longer shall we tell ourselves, "I haven't the time." Rather, our reaction will be, "Now, now, I'm not that busy. I'll offer myself and leave it to Jesus to find me the time." He will.

A sharpened alertness to the needs of others, a sense of sympathy and concern for others, a desire to do something for others, and a hunger to prove my love for Jesus by extending my love to my neighbor are the qualities that become one who truly is Christ's.

Chapter Sixteen

&

Strive to win souls for Christ

❧

How many converts did you win to the Faith during the past year? During the past ten years? During your lifetime? Is there a single person of whom you can truthfully say, "I am the one who brought that person into the Church"?

Just think what it would mean to the kingdom of God if each of us were to make only one convert per year! That does not seem too high a goal when we remember that the first Christians, each of them, made converts by the dozen and by the hundreds. For some reason, we seem to be lacking in the zeal, the dynamism, that a living faith should manifest.

Too many Catholics think that winning converts to the Faith is a job for priests alone. Nothing could be farther from the truth. On Ascension Thursday it was to *all* of us, and not just to the Apostles, that Jesus gave the command "You shall be witnesses for me . . . even to the very ends of the earth."[25] It is true that the final instructing of converts and their actual reception into the Church must be done by priests. However, very few of our too-few converts were won over exclusively by

[25] Acts 1:8.

a priest's preaching or persuasion. In nine out of ten cases, a convert's initial interest in the Catholic Church was inspired by the influence of some Catholic friend or acquaintance.

We all are familiar with the sect known as Jehovah's Witnesses. We tend to be critical of their overly aggressive tactics, and we feel saddened to see them expending so much effort on a mistaken idea of religion. Yet, wrong as they may be on many points, there is one central truth that the Witnesses have absorbed far better than most Catholics: that we are called — all of us — to be witnesses of Jehovah. Every one of us has a positive vocation to be a missionary.

꼭

Work to build up Christ's Mystical Body

Our vocation began with our Baptism. It was then that we became incorporated in Christ, became a cell of His Mystical Body. It is characteristic of a healthy cell to contribute to the health and well-being of the entire body. We are ineffective cells in the Body of Christ if we do not have an urge to contribute to the growth of that Body, if we do not make an effort to add other cells to the Body.

Moreover, in Baptism we became sharers in the priesthood of Jesus. We received the power to offer, with Him, acceptable worship to God. Certainly one of the most powerful ways in which we can offer worship to God is to bring other souls to Him. God's whole concern, humanly speaking, is that men should know and love Him.

Our vocation to be a missionary was formalized and implemented in the sacrament of Confirmation. This sacrament gave us an added share in the priesthood of Jesus. It made us sharers in Christ's *teaching* office, sharers in what the theologians call Christ's prophetic office. The character that was impressed upon our soul in Confirmation gives us a positive *power* for sharing with others the truths of Faith. It gives us a facility in winning others to Christ. And along with the power goes the grace. When we undertake to explain our Faith to others, there is available to us whatever grace we may need in order to do a good job in our efforts at persuasion.

In giving us the sacrament of Confirmation, Jesus did not intend to make us strong in our faith just for our personal benefit. It is the intention of Jesus that through our strength others should find salvation. Jesus gives us the Holy Spirit so that, through our supernatural wisdom, others may become wise in the truths of God. Once we have been confirmed, it is at our peril that we neglect to use our missionary powers.

Don't be afraid to share your Faith with others
"Yes, but I *am* interested in seeing the Church grow," we may say. "I contribute generously to mission collections, and every day I pray for the missions." This is good; this is essential. Yet it does not completely discharge our obligation. We still have the duty to attempt to bring to Christ that man or woman with whom we live or work or recreate. Why is it, then, that so many Catholics seem to neglect their missionary vocation?

With some, it may be due to a greatly mistaken feeling of inferiority. They are afraid they do not know enough about their religion to discuss it with a non-Catholic. If we truly are ignorant and do nothing to dispel our ignorance, we convict ourselves of spiritual laziness or indifference. Either would be a dangerous defense to offer to our Lord on Judgment Day.

However, I feel sure that many Catholics tend to exaggerate their religious ignorance. Such Catholics should suppress their feelings of inferiority in the field of religious knowledge. They certainly know more about religion than does the average non-Catholic they are likely to meet. There may be some answers they do not know, but the answers they do know will be ample to arouse the interest of any well-disposed unbeliever.

Perhaps our reluctance to exercise our missionary powers stems from human respect rather than from feelings of inferiority. We may fear that we shall be rebuffed if we mention religion to a non-Catholic acquaintance. In most instances, this is a totally false fear. Occasionally we may encounter a person so aggressive in his own religious beliefs or so uneasy in his conscience that he resents any discussion of religion. These, however, will be the exceptions. The average non-Catholic is interested in hearing about the Catholic Faith, if only out of plain curiosity. Almost anytime you say, "This is what I believe . . . " you will find your listener following your explanation with receptive attention.

Then, aside from curiosity, there are any number of persons whose own religious ideas are vague and unformed. Being intelligent persons, they experience periods of deep self-questioning: "What is the purpose of life? Why am I here? Where am I headed? How am I doing?" Persons such as these not only do not resent, but actually welcome a discussion of the Catholic

Faith. We make a great mistake if we abstain from speaking of religion for fear that we may offend our hearer. Very often he is just waiting for us to bring up the topic.

Perhaps we would not be so reluctant to broach the subject of religion if we realized that a friend may be pleased by, rather than resentful of, our interest in his spiritual life. If we invite a non-Catholic friend to attend Mass or an inquiry class with us, he is more likely to be pleased than offended. After all, it is a mark of particularly warm friendship to share with another what is most precious to you. We may be surprised at the alacrity with which our invitation is accepted.

You are a Catholic. You have been baptized and confirmed. You have a definite and inescapable vocation to be a missionary to the people around you. If you have been neglectful of this vocation, right now would be the logical time to make a resolution: "During the next twelve months, with the help of God's grace, I am going to bring at least one person into the Church." If you make that resolution and act on it, you will embark upon an exhilarating experience. You may even be amazed to discover that it is so easy. You never had thought of yourself as a missionary. You had even shrunk from any mention of religion. And now, with just a little effort, you find yourself introducing that non-Catholic friend of yours to your pastor.

How should you go about it? Sometimes the direct approach is the best: to ask, over a cup of coffee or a bottle of beer, "Did you ever think of becoming a Catholic?" That simple question can often lead to a fruitful discussion. It may even lead to a course of instructions in the Catholic Faith. Sometimes an invitation to accompany you to Mass (with a preliminary explanation of the significance and the structure of the Mass) is the best beginning. If inquiry classes are conducted in your parish, a suggestion that your friend accompany you to a class will be a very natural beginning — and attendance at the class may be very profitable to you as well.

Your own ingenuity will find many other ways to begin your missionary endeavors, once you awaken to the fact that *you have a missionary vocation*. And you will proceed with confidence, inspired by the fact that it is God's own truth, and not some pet theory of your own, that you are seeking to impart. Your confidence will be doubly reinforced by the knowledge that God is even more interested than you in the conversion of this person. At every step of the way, God's grace will be bombarding the soul of your friend, seeking to find entrance there for the gift of faith you are seeking to share.

If you will begin your missionary vocation, you will have an interesting answer to give if, twelve months from now, someone asks you, "How many converts did you win to the Faith during the past year?" Perhaps no other human will ask, but certainly our Lord will be waiting eagerly for the answer.

Chapter Seventeen

Let love diminish your fear of death

⚭

Are you afraid to die? If you wake up at night with palpitations of the heart or a feeling of suffocation, do you grow panicky at the thought that you may be dying? If you have a narrow escape from an automobile crash, do you feel weak and shaken, perhaps for hours afterward? When you pass the scene of an accident and see a corpse stretched out beside the road, do you feel a chill at this brutal reminder of your own life's frailty? When a friend or relative dies, is a part of your depression occasioned by a renewed consciousness of your own inevitable date with the undertaker?

If your answer to these questions is yes, you may relax: you are a perfectly normal human being. The fear of death — the *wholesome* fear of death — is a built-in mechanism God has provided us with, to ensure that we shall live our allotted span of years. If it were not for this fear, we humans would take more physical risks than we do. We would have much less care of our health than we do. Adequate safeguarding of our lives is an obligation that God imposes on us in His Fifth Commandment.[26]

---

[26] "Thou shalt not kill" (Exod. 20:13).

But God has made the keeping of this commandment easier for everyone by providing us with that fear of death which we more commonly call "the instinct of self-preservation."

Anxiety concerning death is intensified by our natural shrinking from the thought of the pain that, for many of us, must precede death.

Another element of our anxiety stems from our fear of the unknown. Faith tells us that Heaven may not be *too* different from life as we know it. Will I to some extent lose my present identity in Heaven? Will it be the present *I* who enjoys this happiness? Our reaction to Heaven is something like that of the icebound Eskimo who is told of the wonders of life in the temperate zone. He listens to the description of sunshine and warmth, of beautiful flowers and trees and singing birds, of delicious meats and vegetables, fruits and desserts. He shakes his head doubtfully and asks, "Can I get seal blubber there?" We have a sneaking reluctance to leave our earthly enjoyments for the poorly understood bliss of eternity, a reluctance dispelled only by a lively faith.

While a healthy fear of death is a quite normal human emotion, there is an unhealthy fear, a morbid fear, of death from which an occasional person may suffer. One who suffers from this morbid fear is likely to be preoccupied with the thought of death, much too anxious about illness and possible accidents, much too disturbed at encounters with death, possibly to the point of being unable to look at a corpse or even to attend a wake. Such unwholesome fear may have resulted from a severely traumatic event in childhood or may represent an unconscious defense against repressed suicidal impulses.

Let love diminish your fear of death

Such morbid fear may need the aid of a psychiatrist for its relief and is outside the scope of our discussion here.

Since a fear of death is an emotional reaction common to all of us, it follows that this fear is not an accurate gauge of our spiritual state. Fear of death is not the same thing as fear of Hell. We may feel as sure as we humanly can that we are living habitually in the state of grace, yet still experience this natural shrinking from the prospect of death. Emotions are not something we can turn on or off like a water faucet. Emotions do not respond easily to the discipline of reason or even to the discipline of faith.

We encounter persons who seem to feel that there is something shameful about being afraid to die, as though a good person, a person of faith, should have no fear of death. When such a person boasts that he is not afraid to die, it is likely that either he has never had a close personal brush with death and so has never awakened his fear, or his fear of death is too intense for him to face; he must whistle in order to keep up his courage.

But, if fear of death is such a universal characteristic of normal humans, why have the saints seemed so immune to this fear? St. Paul eagerly looked forward to his death; he prayed that he might be dissolved and be with Christ.[27] St. Lawrence and St. Thomas More[28] joked with their executioners. The early martyrs went, singing joyfully, to face the wild beasts in

[27] Cf. Phil. 1:23.

[28] St. Lawrence (d. 258), deacon and martyr; St. Thomas More (1478-1535), Lord Chancellor of England and martyr.

the arena. It would seem that fear of death is incompatible with high sanctity.

Yet that is not quite true. With the saints, it is not a matter of stifling fear as an unworthy weakness; it is rather a case of a lesser emotion paling before a stronger one, as the rising sun vanquishes the light of the moon. It is not necessarily that the saints have any less fear of the physical fact of death than you or I do; it is rather that for them the fact of death becomes all but forgotten in their eagerness for the full possession of God.

Not long ago I heard of a child who ran right through a glass door to throw himself into the arms of his father, whom he spied getting out of a cab. The father was returning from a long business trip, and the child, in his eagerness for reunion, forgot all about the door. He wasn't even conscious of his cuts until the disturbed father called attention to them. More than once, too, we have read of parents who have rushed through searing flames, oblivious to their own burns, in order to rescue a threatened child. In all such instances, one strong emotion, fear, has been totally eclipsed by a stronger emotion, love. Obstacles or threats have ceased to matter because of what lies beyond. If love has not cast out fear, at least it has made fear completely unimportant.

Perhaps now we can ask the question: How should a Christian die?

Ideally we ought, all of us, to die like saints — that is, to look forward to Heaven with eyes so full of hunger for God that there is no glance left for the forbidding door of death that stands between. If at present we fall short of such love, there is no reason we should remain reconciled to our mediocrity. God is eager to lead us on to greater love if only we will show a willingness to be led.

❧

Learn to grow in love for God

This will mean that a great part of our prayers will be devoted to a petition for growth in love. It will mean, too, that we exercise ourselves in love by practicing love on our neighbor. It is not only true that we show our love for God by our love for our neighbors; it also is true that love shown to our neighbor is the best possible technique for growth in love for God. Every deliberate act of kindness, forgiveness, unselfishness, compassion, consideration, patience, and helpfulness will bring in its train greater love for God. If you are doubtful, just try it for a week. At the end of seven days, you will see that God is more real to you, more vividly present, and more perceptibly an object of your love.

We also can increase our hunger for God by reading about and meditating on the nature of God and on what it will mean to see Him face-to-face. Newspapers, magazines, and TV fill our leisure hours and our heads with knowledge that has but a passing value. The knowledge that is of most vital importance too often remains untasted. We may know more about the intimate life of the queen of England than we know about the nature of God; more about the politics of South Africa than about the joys of Heaven. Too many of us leave spiritual reading to nuns and priests, as though they were the only ones destined for death and eternity.

We cannot love Him whom we do not know, and we cannot know Him without the effort of learning. If our concept of Heaven is still our child's-eye view of grade-school days, it is little wonder that our gaze is not drawn above and beyond the barrier of death. In our mature years we have learned much about the nature of love — what it means to love and to be loved. Yet we may still be thinking of Heaven in vague and abstract terms. If so, such phrases as "seeing God" and "being united with God" can leave us unexcited and unmoved.

We need to rouse ourselves to an understanding of what it will mean to be caught up in the cyclonic embrace of Absolute Love; that intensely personal one-to-one love in which I am all God's and He is all mine; a union in which my soul goes out to God in one great explosive burst of love such as I had never known myself capable of; the fusion of God and me, in which the power of God's love for me all but tears me apart in a climax of almost painful ecstasy. When I have grasped something of the real nature of God and of Heaven, then will the grim and forbidding face of death begin to soften and to lose its terror.

❧

Offer even your death to God

While we are growing in the love and eagerness for God that will leapfrog the thought of death, we can turn our very fear of death into an instrument of love. It was by sin that death came into the world. We can turn death against itself by offering our fear of death as an atonement for sin — for our own sins and for all the sins of the world that pinioned Christ to the Cross.

Let love diminish your fear of death

In our moments of anxiety about death, we can range ourselves beside Jesus in Gethsemane as He makes the tortured offering of His life to the Father. He did it in order that my own death might be, in the end, a victory rather than a defeat. I can unite my own will with that of Jesus and make my offering with His: "Thy will be done, O God. In my death, Thy blessed will be done!" In this act of accepting and offering my death to God, this act of "dying in advance," I have done much to weaken my human repugnance to death.

Recognizing the value of such a practice, the Church grants for this practice a plenary indulgence that will be effective in the very moment of death. Here are the words of the grant:

> The faithful who at any time in their lives, from a sincere spirit of love of God and with at least a contrite heart, express their intention of accepting calmly and gladly from the hand of God whatsoever manner of death it may please Him to send them, together with all its pain, anguish and suffering, may gain an indulgence of seven years (each time the offering is made) and a plenary indulgence at the hour of death, if they have devoutly made such an act at least once in their lifetime, after having fulfilled the usual conditions.

For gaining a plenary indulgence the "usual conditions" are Confession, Holy Communion, and at least one Our Father, Hail Mary, and Glory Be for the intentions of the Pope. The usual conditions need be fulfilled only once for the plenary indulgence. The act of offering our death, however, with its partial indulgence, should be repeated as often as the thought of death comes into our mind.

Christ calms the fears of the dying

Whenever I speak or write of death, I think of Mrs. Lemay's last Holy Communion. Mrs. Lemay, a gentle, white-haired lady with pink satin cheeks and bright blue eyes, had been an invalid in her daughter's home for several months and had been anointed several times. As I came into her room this particular morning, she smiled a greeting that was intended both for me and for Him whom I carried with me. Propped up on her pillows, she received Holy Communion with her usual eagerness, answering all the prayers in a clear voice. As I pronounced the concluding blessing, she relaxed and closed her eyes. After I had purified the pyx, I asked her, as I always did, how she was feeling. It took a few moments for her daughter and me to realize that Mrs. Lemay was dead, so gently had she slipped away from us. She already was gazing upon the visible Christ whom just a moment ago she had received under the appearance of bread. No one could illustrate better than Mrs. Lemay how a Christian ought to die.

As we think nervously of death, it is encouraging to know that Mrs. Lemay's death is typical rather than exceptional. I do not mean to say that all good Christians die as quickly as she or that all are fortunate enough to die immediately after receiving Holy Communion. What I do say is that in my thirty-three years of experience as a priest, I have never — I repeat, *never* — seen a good Catholic in fear of death when the moment of death actually came. I have seen many who were very apprehensive about death up until the time of receiving the Anointing of the Sick, but with the holy anointing, apprehension disappears. To see the change that takes place in timorous hearts after receiving the Anointing of the Sick is like watching a miracle.

To ensure the continuance of the human race, God has given us an instinctive resistance to the thought of death and to the pains that may precede it. In His goodness, however, God erases this resistance and fear when the time of death actually comes. And, for whatever measure of pain He may permit before death, God gives a corresponding increase in courage and stamina. I half-suspect that the first thought that will cross our mind as our soul catapults from its worn-out body into the embrace of God will be "Why, it wasn't hard to die at all!"

How should a Christian die? If he is truly a Christian, he not only should but *shall* die in one last act of faith and hope: faith that death is but the entrance to the real life for which he was created; hope in the infinite mercy of God, who is content with so little from us. Death will be an act of love, too: a loving acceptance of God's plan for us and God's will. But death will not be a last act of love. Faith and hope must end with death, their duty done. But love, such love as we have never dreamed of, is just beginning.

Biographical Note

❧

Leo J. Trese
(1902-1970)

※

"Christ's whole life was one of concern for others," wrote Leo Trese — and this humble priest dedicated his own life to showing that same concern. Through more than forty years of priestly ministry, Leo Trese poured himself out for Christ's flock and wrote numerous clear, spiritually rich books to inform, inspire, and encourage Christians worldwide.

Born in Port Huron, Michigan, Leo Trese was ordained a priest of the Archdiocese of Detroit in 1927 and served as associate and as pastor at various parishes in Michigan. Concern for the least fortunate marked his priestly ministry from the beginning, moving him to make time to serve as chaplain at an assisted-living residence for women and as chaplain for a school. In 1936 he was named the first pastor of St. Christopher Church in Marysville, Michigan, as well as of the Mexican Center in Port Huron, Michigan. He was so dedicated to his pastoral work that he received permission to spend a brief period in El Paso, Texas, in order to study Spanish so he could better serve the Mexican population in Michigan.

In the 1940s, Fr. Trese began receiving so many requests for spiritual guidance that he started to write spiritual books to provide direction in the most comprehensive and straight-forward manner possible. His writing quickly grew from a hobby that he pursued in his spare time to an apostolate that consumed most of his energies. Soon he was receiving numer-ous requests to give retreats and radio talks.

By 1953 the demand for his writings had become so great that Fr. Trese became concerned that writing was interfering with his care for his parishioners. He still wrote only to fulfill specific requests, but those requests had multiplied tremen-dously. "Maybe it is God's will," he told Detroit's Archbishop, Edward Cardinal Mooney. "If I say no, I may be refusing Him the little talent He has given me." As a loyal son of the Church, he asked Cardinal Mooney to decide whether he could better serve as a priest by ceasing to write or by being re-lieved of some of his pastoral duties. Recognizing the value of Fr. Trese's writing, the diocese granted him several leaves so that he could devote his time solely to spiritual writing.

In addition to articles for magazines such as *Ave Maria*, Fr. Trese wrote numerous books on spirituality, apologetics, the priesthood, and even child psychology. Among his best works are *A Man Approved, Vessel of Clay, You Are Called to Great-ness, Many Are One, Book for Boys, Parent and Child*, and his enduringly popular *The Faith Explained*. Demand for his writ-ings has never abated: his works have spread throughout the world and have been translated into Spanish, German, French, Italian, and Korean. Suffused with clarity, warm humor, and simple, down-to-earth examples, Fr. Trese's books continue to help today's readers to know and love the Catholic Faith, and to inspire them to live it out in all circumstances.